# Leading Corporate
# Turnaround

# Leading Corporate Turnaround

## How Leaders Fix Troubled Companies

Stuart Slatter
David Lovett
Laura Barlow

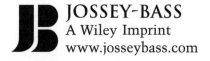
JOSSEY-BASS
A Wiley Imprint
www.josseybass.com

Published by      John Wiley & Sons Ltd, The Atrium, Southern Gate, Chichester,
West Sussex PO19 8SQ, England

Telephone    (+44) 1243 779777

Under the Jossey-Bass imprint, Jossey-Bass 989, Market Street, San Francisco CA 94103-1741 USA
www.jossey-bass.com

Email (for orders and customer service enquiries): cs-books@wiley.co.uk
Visit our Home Page on www.wiley.com

Reprinted April 2006, September 2006, March 2008

**Other Wiley Editorial Offices**

John Wiley & Sons Inc., 111 River Street, Hoboken, NJ 07030, USA

Jossey-Bass, 989 Market Street, San Francisco, CA 94103-1741, USA

Wiley-VCH Verlag GmbH, Boschstr. 12, D-69469 Weinheim, Germany

John Wiley & Sons Australia Ltd, 42 McDougall Street, Milton, Queensland 4064, Australia

John Wiley & Sons (Asia) Pte Ltd, 2 Clementi Loop #02-01, Jin Xing Distripark, Singapore 129809

John Wiley & Sons Canada Ltd, 22 Worcester Road, Etobicoke, Ontario, Canada M9W 1L1

Wiley also publishes its books in a variety of electronic formats. Some content that appears
in print may not be available in electronic books.

**Library of Congress Cataloging-in-Publication Data**

Slatter, Stuart St. P.
    Leading corporate turnaround : how leaders fix troubled companies /
Stuart Slatter, David Lovett, and Laura Barlow.
       p.   cm.
    Includes index.
    ISBN 978-0-470-02559-8
    1. Corporate turnarounds – Management.   2. Leadership.   I. Lovett, David.
II. Barlow, Laura.   III. Title.
    HD58.8.S58 2006
    658.4′092 – dc22                                              2005027090

**British Library Cataloguing in Publication Data**

A catalogue record for this book is available from the British Library

ISBN   978-0-470-02559-8 (HB)


Typeset in 11/13pt Plantin by TechBooks, New Delhi, India
Printed and bound in Great Britain by TJ International Ltd, Padstow, Cornwall, UK
This book is printed on acid-free paper.

# Contents

# About the Authors

**Stuart Slatter** Founding partner of Stuart Slatter & Company, Chairman of Stuart Slatter Training and a Visiting Fellow in Strategic and International Management at the London Business School (LBS).

Stuart Slatter has over twenty-five years of experience in providing strategic consultancy advice and management education to senior management throughout the world. While a full time faculty member at LBS, he was Dean for Executive Education, Director of the Senior Executive Programme, and Chairman of the Strategic and International Management Department. He has been a Visiting Professor at the University of California (UCLA) and at the University of Capetown. Prior to joining LBS, he was Managing Director of a subsidiary of a UK public company, and a senior management consultant with Booz, Allen & Hamilton in New York specialising in marketing strategy.

He holds a law degree from Cambridge University, an MBA degree from Stanford Business School, and a PhD in marketing from London University. He is a qualified barrister-at-law, and is the author of a number of books and articles, including "Gambling on Growth", Wiley (1992), and "Corporate Turnaround", Penguin Books (1999). He was one of the founding directors of the Society of Turnaround Professionals in the UK, and can be contacted via www.slatter.co.uk.

**David C. Lovett** David Lovett, a Managing Director with AlixPartners and a member of the European Executive group of the firm, is a business graduate, a fellow of the Institute of Chartered Accountants of England and Wales, a fellow and a founding member of the

Society of Turnaround Professionals. Before joining AlixPartners, David was with Andersen for 18 years, where he formed Andersen's London-based turnaround practice in the early 1990s and subsequently led the Global Turnaround practice. He co-authored "Corporate Turnaround" with Stuart Slatter in 1999.

During the last 30 years, David has advised all the classes of stakeholders in troubled companies. He has led many corporate restructurings and turnarounds in both an advisory and officer capacity serving as Chief Financial Officer and Chief Restructuring Officer.

David has extensive cross border restructuring experience and is familiar with the changing trends in insolvency and restructuring legislation. He is driven by a desire to minimise economic loss to stakeholders while his clients manage the turbulence of forced transformation.

AlixPartners is recognised internationally as the "industry standard" for solving complex business challenges, helping companies improve operating and financial performance, and restoring corporate value. Founded in 1981, it has been retained by hundreds of companies throughout the USA, Europe, Asia and Latin America and has worked in virtually all industries and sectors.

**Laura Barlow** Laura Barlow is a Director in AlixPartners' European Turnaround and Restructuring practice. Over the past 15 years she has been an adviser to both creditors and debtors in troubled situations and has worked with numerous companies to help them achieve operational turnaround and financial restructuring. She has taken interim management roles in several troubled companies, restoring stability and leading the development and implementation of turnaround plans. Her current focus is on providing restructuring advisory services to corporates, including taking Chief Restructuring Officer positions where appropriate.

Laura is a graduate of Oxford University, a Chartered Accountant and SFA Securities Representative. She is a regular speaker at European conferences on turnaround and restructuring and at the London Business School on the Managing Corporate Turnarounds course.

# Acknowledgements

The research for this book was only made possible through the co-operation of the Society for Turnaround Professionals (STP) in the UK. Ian McIsaac of Deloittes and John Harris, who were respectively the Chairman and Chief Executive of STP when the research commenced, were most supportive and encouraged STP members to participate. The Appendix provides more details about STP.

Sixty members of STP and twenty other leading turnaround practitioners were interviewed by students on the MBA and Sloan programmes at London Business School (LBS) during the spring and summer of 2003. We would like to thank all those individuals for the generous amount of time they gave to talk to the LBS students. We have only named a few of those interviewed in the book although the quotes are taken from a wide cross section of those interviewed. The students who undertook the interviews did so as part of an extremely popular course on Managing Corporate Turnarounds, which is taught by Stuart Slatter at the London Business School. We are extremely grateful for their efforts and analysis.

We have also drawn heavily on the experiences of Chairmen and Chief Executives who have come as guest speakers to the Managing Corporate Turnaround course at LBS over recent years and to bankers, private equity players, AlixPartners, and other senior executives who have given generously of their time in conversation with us. Two colleagues at AlixPartners, Peter Fitzsimmons and Lisa Donahue, were particularly helpful in sharing the applicability of their transatlantic perspectives to the European markets. We should emphasize that the views and opinions expressed in this book do not necessarily state or reflect those of AlixPartners, Ltd. or its worldwide affiliates and employees.

We are hugely indebted to the leaders who took time out of their busy schedules to read the manuscript and provide us with their comments for the cover of the book.

Barbara Meade of Stuart Slatter Training and Petra de Souza Thomson of AlixPartners have been wonderful in preparing the manuscript, working tirelessly and cheerfully on it while juggling other priorities.

# Introduction

THIS BOOK EXPLORES THE ROLE OF LEADERSHIP IN CORPORATE turnarounds based on interviews with over 80 turnaround practitioners (75% of whom are members of the Society of Turnaround Professionals in the UK and our collective experiences as advisers to companies in trouble. The book does not set out to develop any new theories of leadership but seeks to describe how leadership is provided by turnaround practitioners throughout the turnaround process.

In our earlier book, *Corporate Turnaround* (Penguin Books 1999)* we identified seven key ingredients that characterise a successful turnaround, and described *what* turnaround practitioners need to do to rescue a distressed company. We have taken this same framework – described in Chapter 2 – and looked at *how* leading turnaround practitioners provide leadership for each of these ingredients (Chapters 4 to 10). In the course of our research we discovered that good leadership is critical even before the start of the turnaround – often many months in advance – since stakeholder commitment to the turnaround process must be obtained before any turnaround can begin. Chapter 3 explores how leadership is provided at this stage of the process.

There is often a debate about where turnaround ends. Is it after stabilisation? Is it after refocusing and fixing the business? Or is it after rejuvenating the company and embedding a new organisational culture? Our definition of a turnaround stops short of the latter although, as we will see in the book, a few turnaround leaders are able to adapt their leadership style towards the needs of longer term transformation and growth. What is clear is that the leadership style necessary in the early stages of a turnaround is not appropriate for the

---

* Published as *Corporate Recovery* in the USA. (Beard 2004).

transformation challenge of building a sustainable organisation in the longer term.

The emphasis on survival early in the turnaround process implies the need to achieve rapid performance improvement, usually within a 6 to 18 month time frame, and sometimes even sooner. The need to deliver short-term results is what turnaround practitioners focus on; leaving the longer term success of the company to a subsequent leader.

Our experience in advising companies that need to change but are not in financial distress leads us to believe that the book has wide implications for all managers whether or not their organisation is in crisis. If under-performance is the problem and rapid improvement in financial performance is required by the key stakeholder(s), then the leadership approach used by turnaround practitioners is required to achieve results. This is what happened at Gillette between 2001 and 2003 when a new chairman/CEO, Jim Kilts, was brought in to improve performance. The actions he took and the leadership styles he used were "textbook" turnaround even though Gillette was not in a financial crisis.

We would go one step further and say that in any business where there is a recognised need for transformation, because the current success formula is approaching the end of its life, the transformation process will not take root unless it is kick-started by the type of leadership approach used by turnaround leaders. Most corporate transformation efforts fail because there is no sense of urgency for immediate results, and senior management is not willing or capable of adopting a short-term, results-oriented leadership style.

Leading change, which this book is about, is an enormous topic and has been the subject of many good books. However our focus is on radical short-term change which delivers fast financial gain. We believe that the book we have produced here on leading corporate turnaround is a major contribution that is easy to read. We hope you will enjoy it.

# 1

# The Leadership Challenge

TURNAROUND PRACTITIONERS ARE MORE OFTEN ASSOCIATED with ruthless "downsizing" rather than the more inspiring concept of leadership. Yet leadership is never more important than when survival is at stake, and corporate turnarounds are no exception. Management skills are a critical ingredient but exceptional leadership is required at nearly all stages of the turnaround process if a sustainable turnaround is to be achieved.

There are many difficult leadership challenges facing the turnaround practitioner, particularly the turnaround executive (usually a new chairman or CEO) who has the ultimate responsibility for achieving the turnaround of a distressed corporate. He or she faces all or most of the following challenges:

- Convincing the key stakeholders that turnaround is the best option for recovering value in the distressed company.

- "Grabbing hold" or taking control of the company so that all stakeholders and particularly the staff realise that new leadership is in place.

- Changing management as appropriate and building a new management team to support the turnaround.

- Instilling an immediate sense of urgency and performance orientation into the distressed company.

- Implementing tight management and financial controls.

- Developing and communicating a vision for the business and obtaining ownership and buy-in to the vision by managers and employees.

- Prioritising what needs to be done to fix the business, and ensuring that the necessary actions are implemented.

- Rebuilding the organisation's effectiveness which is likely to involve embedding a new culture into the business.

- Providing ongoing stakeholder management, including leading a financial restructuring of the corporate entity.

## Turnaround Practioners

We find that leadership is provided in turnaround situations by turnaround executives, financial stakeholders (both equity owners and creditors), advisers and occasionally by interim managers. Recently a new category of turnaround leader has emerged, the Chief Restructuring Officer (CRO), who is usually an adviser but will assume line management and Board level responsibility for specific aspects of the turnaround. We will look at each briefly in turn.

### Turnaround Executives

Popularly known by journalists as company doctors, these individuals take executive responsibility in the distressed company. They usually come in as chairman or chief executive officer, and have full authority to take decisions within the limits imposed or agreed by the controlling stakeholder(s), who are either the debtors (the equity owners) or the creditors (usually the bankers or increasingly specialist funds that hold debt in distressed companies). Sometimes the turnaround professional is brought in as deputy chairman or chief operating officer – as in a family-owned business for example – but if he or she is to do the job, then that individual is de facto the chief executive.

### Financial Stakeholders

Although shareholders and in particular banks almost never have or want executive responsibility (except perhaps in an owner-managed business where the shareholders are also executives), they often play a key leadership role in triggering the start of a successful turnaround process. The reader will see examples of this in Chapter 3, when we talk about the decision to undertake a turnaround; and again in Chapter 10 on financial restructuring. Private equity houses, mezzanine funders, banks and specialist recovery funds play bigger leadership roles in turnarounds than many observers realise, particularly given the rapid growth in secondary debt trading and distressed asset investment in recent years.

## Advisers

Until recently corporate recovery departments of accounting firms often played a leadership role in galvanising incumbent management to take action – usually when there was a leadership void and occasionally they provided leadership in a specific area such as cash management or financial restructuring where they had specialist expertise that did not exist within the incumbent management team. The increased regulation of accounting firms following the corporate governance failures predominantly in the USA has resulted in these firms reconsidering their service offering with the result that the number of specialist advisory firms who perform this work has grown considerably. Specialist teams within certain investment banks are increasingly involved with the balance sheet restructuring work that was once the preserve of the corporate recovery departments.

## Chief Restructuring Officer

This is a relatively new corporate role which first emerged in the USA and is now gaining popularity in Europe. The Chief Restructuring Officer (CRO) is always an experienced recovery professional who focuses on crisis stabilisation, stakeholder management and financial restructuring.

The CRO usually acts as a special adviser to the chairman, CEO or Board with responsibility for leading whatever financial restructuring is necessary – first, to allow a turnaround to take place and, second, to ensure that there is an appropriate financial structure for the longer term. The demand for the services of a CRO reflects the increasing complexity of capital structures even in mid-sized corporates, and therefore of the financial restructuring process. It is also a recognition that many turnaround executives, while capable chairmen or CEOs, lack the expertise – and indeed the time – to lead a complex financial restructuring in parallel with an operational turnaround. The CRO is not a permanent position, but while working with the company he or she becomes central to everything that is occuring.

The appointment of a CRO is increasingly a precondition of support by financial stakeholders who need this aspect of the turnaround to be led by an experienced restructuring practitioner.

### Interim Managers

Short-term management resources are sometimes introduced by the turnaround executive to deal with immediate business problems, particularly if radical changes are immediately required in the senior management layer. Sometimes these interim managers are part of a "commando" team who move around with a turnaround executive. They sometimes provide functional leadership but their role is primarily to bring experience to the management of critical tasks.

## Turnaround Executives: What they Do and Who they Are

There is a wide spectrum of capabilities among turnaround executives. While we advocate that the complete turnaround leader should be able to lead and manage all the critical ingredients that make up a good turnaround, the reality is that many do not have the desire or capability (or both) to lead all aspects of the process. This is not in itself a bad thing. They are all experienced, confident individuals who know their limitations which in itself is an attribute of good leadership.

What we see in practice is a spectrum of turnaround executives ranging from those who specialise in crisis stabilisation to those who undertake the complete turnaround and are prepared to stay on after the turnaround is complete to lead future growth and organisational transformation. All turnaround professionals undertake crisis stabilisation, but relatively few have the desire or capability to continue once the company has been returned to a stable condition. The particular skills and attributes of the typical turnaround executive (as discussed in the next section) do not fit with the needs of steady-state or growing organisations.

We see a sharp distinction between the turnaround executive who only does crisis stabilisation work and is rarely in a company for more than 6 to 12 months (and many for as little as three months), and the turnaround executive who does the stabilisation and also fixes the critical underlying problems of the business. This takes longer and is likely to involve leadership over at least a 12- to 24-month period.

The crisis stabilisation specialists will take management control, implement strict cash and cost controls, negotiate with the key stakeholders and change a few key managers at the top. Their aim is to ensure not only the short-term survival of the business but also that there is a management team in place who can fix the business problems that caused the crisis in the first place. These turnaround executives often have a financial background, and many have worked in their early careers in the insolvency profession. They stick to what they are good at – managing financial crises – and believe that the business should be fixed by managers who know the industry and are going to be responsible for its future performance.

The complete turnaround executive, as we like to call that person, believes that a turnaround is not complete unless and until the underlying causes of distress have been dealt with. He or she believes – and we agree – that an effective turnaround usually requires strategic refocusing, critical process improvements and some degree of organisational change if the business is not to revert into a turnaround situation. Not surprisingly many turnaround executives fall somewhere between the two "types" we have described – they initiate and lead strategic change and critical business process improvements to rectify the business problems, but do not participate too deeply in all the detailed management activities that are necessary to effect a complete turnaround.

In a large organisation, particularly one with many diversified business units, the turnaround leader operating at the corporate level would not be expected to be involved in detailed competitive strategy analysis and process improvements (although many do in practice). However, in smaller companies, where it is more difficult to have good-quality senior managers, it is extremely risky to delegate responsibility for making decisions that are critical to the success of the turnaround. Although the senior managers may know their industry, their analytical and decision-making skills may be woefully inadequate. Furthermore, their capability to implement change throughout the organisation is still likely to be weak, unless a sufficient critical mass of new high-quality middle managers has been brought in. This is particularly the case where the previous leader or CEO was highly autocratic and senior management are not accustomed to managing change.

Who are the individuals that work as turnaround executives or company doctors? They are a relatively small group of experienced executives who at some stage in their career – out of choice or serendipity (but usually the latter) – became involved in managing a company in financial distress. Having done it once they become hooked on the buzz, the challenge and the adrenalin rush that comes from turning a company around. Anecdotal evidence suggests that many turnaround executives are unemployable in a large company environment, since they are quickly frustrated by what they see as bureaucracy and slow decision making. They are tough, competitive individuals with enormous will power, who "call a spade a spade" and "are happy to take on anybody who wants a fight". They are also "loners" who do not need or want social relationships in the workplace. As one executive put it:

> "I don't need friends at work . . . respect will do very nicely thank you."

This is at the heart of leadership. Leadership is not about being loved by everyone: it is about being understood and respected by enough people to get the job done.

We have been fortunate to have had access to a piece of proprietary research carried out to look at the psychological characteristics of leading turnaround executives in the UK. It shows remarkable consistency with the anecdotal evidence in that the vast majority of turnaround executives are logical, objective decision makers, who are very task focused and want to control their external environments.

Very few individuals show a tolerance for flexibility and ambiguity. Most want to exert a great deal of control over others' actions and decisions, but do not want anyone else to have control over them! They will happily accept a lot of responsibility – perhaps even over-extending themselves – and are very competitive with both themselves and others. They thrive on authority, responsibility, predictability, stability and consistency. Ambiguity and change are tolerated only to the extent that this is necessary while they return the organisation to a stable state.

Turnaround practitioners are detached and logical, and seen as tough and uncompromising. They like clear objectives, and when they are convinced of something they make it happen. They push people hard to achieve deadlines, can be extremely impatient and do not hesitate to "ruffle feathers" in the process. They do not show much empathy and have a low need to be included in social activities. They prefer not to socialise with work colleagues and are highly selective with whom they choose to interact. They are self-sufficient and exhibit healthy levels of confidence, although most are not charismatic leaders. Another characteristic of turnaround executives is their stamina. Turning a company around is a "24/7 job"; it requires long hours, the ability to work under (often quite extreme) stress and, of course, total commitment. *"I was breathing, living and dreaming about the company for months . . . in a quest for the best solution,"* said one turnaround executive.

Box 1.1 provides a glimpse of how turnaround executives describe themselves.

---

**Box 1.1    How Turnaround Executives Describe Themselves**

- *"Tough, fair and above all decisive."*

- *"Highly communicative, fast acting, trustworthy, inclusive, tough but fair."*

- *"I listen quietly, I tell it straight and then I take action."*

- *"I select a team, I call a spade a spade, I fix the issue, I keep control, I don't expect to be liked, I'm dogged but I get out before I lose the buzz."*

- *"I am matter of fact, straightforward. Don't suffer fools gladly. Detail minded. Like good quality information, like numbers and business propositions. I am quite aggressive and direct."*

- *"Decisive and persistent."*

- *"I am highly communicative, fast acting, trustworthy, inclusive, tough but fair."*

- *"I am quick to get to the point, quick to decide, ruthless in execution, cold and efficient, a hard worker. People who work for me feel included, are informed about what is happening and know what the milestones are."*

## What is Turnaround Leadership?

Turnaround leadership, in broad terms, is the role a person plays in trying to change an organisation for the better. A leader is someone who has the ability to convince others to follow the path he or she decides. Much has been written on the subject of leadership and there is no shortage of options when looking for a definition.

Since this book is about leadership, albeit in the specific context of corporate turnarounds, we need to be clear on how we have defined leadership for the purposes of our research. The definition we like – because it is simple and has been widely accepted – is that used by John Kotter in his seminal book, *Leading Change*, where he describes the difference between management and leadership:

> *"Management is a set of processes that can keep a complicated system of people and technology running smoothly. The most important aspect of management include planning, budgeting, organising, staffing, controlling and problem solving. Leadership is a set of processes that creates organisations in the first place or adapts them to significantly changing circumstances. Leadership defines what the future should look like, aligns people with that vision and inspires them to make it happen despite the obstacles."*

Managers and leaders have different strengths. Richard Kovacevich, chairman and CEO of Wells Fargo Bank, puts it this way:

> *"Managers rely on systems, leaders rely on people. Managers work at getting things right, leaders work on the right things. The answer to every problem, choice or opportunity in our company is known to someone or some team in the company. The leader only has to find that person, listen and help them effect the change."*

Never is this more true than in a corporate turnaround. The answers are usually there within the company but what has been missing is the leadership to deal with the problems the organisation faces. As a turnaround executive put it to us:

> *"You are destined to fail unless you can get the plans you present implemented. . . . It all comes down to leadership . . . it's about people."*

Yet the people you need are often in denial when a crisis hits – not just the management of the distressed firm but sometimes even the financial stakeholders. It is an emotional time: people's behaviour is not always rational. The turnaround leader is the one who has to provide the leadership necessary to bring sense and order to the situation.

Turnaround executives display many of the classic characteristics of good leaders but the big situational difference in turnarounds is that time is of the essence. A conclusion of a recent *Harvard Business Review* article was that "*the (new) CEO must learn to manage organisational context rather than focus on daily operations*". It went on to say that "*the CEO must learn to act in indirect ways . . . to create the conditions that will help others to make the right choices*".* This is fine for a successful business, but such an approach would be completely inappropriate in a turnaround situation. The priority for turnaround executives is to save the company, which means being "very hands on" and extremely focused on three or four mission critical objectives. The need for the turnaround leader to become involved in management detail – even in large companies – is one of the defining features of turnaround

---

* *Harvard Business Review*, 2004.

leadership. The leadership skills required to achieve dramatic short-term change requires the use of several different leadership styles.

While there is a wide range of leadership styles among turnaround executives, virtually all exhibit the following leadership characteristics:

- They quickly develop clear short term priorities and goals.
- They exhibit visible authority.
- They set expectations and enforce standards.
- They are decisive and implement their decisions quickly.
- They communicate continuously with all stakeholders.
- They build confidence and trust by being transparent and honest.
- They adopt an autocratic leadership style during crisis stabilisation.

While it is generally accepted that coercive or autocratic leadership usually has a destructive impact on organisational climate and longer term results – because it restricts the development of people and ideas – the early phases of a turnaround are the exception. Decisions have to be taken very rapidly to ensure survival and there is little time to win over management and staff. Having a new leader take complete charge quickly may come as a relief to much of the workforce if previous management was seen to be weak or if high levels of anxiety exist due to the uncertainty caused by the crisis. Aligning and motivating people to achieve short-term results requires considerably more communication than is normal in a "steady-state" organisation.

While the turnaround leader must take control quickly he or she risks being too aggressive to achieve successful buy in. Success requires decisiveness, clear direction, and a high level of communication, inspiration and motivation. Achieving quick results without being too hard line is an "art", born of considerable situational experience. The leader must achieve a fine balance between gaining co-operation and directing purposeful action to save the company.

The best turnaround leaders are able to develop and articulate a medium to long-term strategic vision for a sustainable recovery and embed a new organisational culture, which ensures that the company does not slip back into crisis. However, the objective of many turnaround situations is not long term sustainable recovery. A high proportion of turnaround situations are sold off after stabilisation or once recovery has started, so the turnaround leader does not need the leadership skills required to bring about true transformation.

## Leading and Managing

In successful organisations, leaders can emerge who are not necessarily good at management but are able to choose good managers to work for them. If good leadership is missing at the top in a successful organisation, good management may be able to keep the business going successfully if major change is not required. However, this does not apply in a turnaround situation.

Turnarounds usually involve a failure of both leadership and management with the result that, at the start of a turnaround, the company lacks both direction and control. If a successful turnaround is to be achieved what is usually required is a quantum leap in performance at the same time as restoring the disciplines necessary to provide predictable results. We believe that it is primarily leadership skills that allow the quantum leap to occur, and management skills that provide the discipline and predictability (see Figure 1.1).

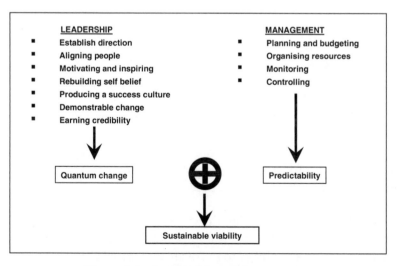

Figure 1.1   Leadership vs Management.

While advisers and interim managers can and do provide some of the management skills necessary in a turnaround, the turnaround executive must be prepared to structure the management detail. As one executive put it, *"they must roll up their sleeves and tackle problems personally"*. This is as true with large companies as it is with small companies. When Gillette brought in a new chairman/CEO – Jim Kilts from Kraft Foods – in 2002, he personally undertook a detailed diagnosis of each business unit on arrival. Every experienced turnaround executive knows that the true financial situation is nearly always worse than the financial stakeholders thought at the start. Only by getting involved in some of the management detail can the turnaround executive be certain he knows what is really happening in the business.

We firmly believe that a good turnaround executive has *both* good leadership and good management skills. In looking at what turnaround practitioners do to deliver the seven key ingredients that characterise successful turnarounds (described in more detail in Chapter 2), we observe that both leadership and management skills are required to varying degrees in all aspects of the turnaround process. We have already mentioned in the Introduction how the need for these skills starts prior to the beginning of the turnaround. In some areas, such as changing management, stakeholder management and organisation development, leadership skills dominate. In other areas, such as implementing controls and critical process improvement, management skills dominate, while in yet others a combination is required.

Figure 1.2 shows our assessment of the relative importance of leadership and management skills throughout the turnaround process.

The fundamental reason why turnarounds require a broad range of management and leadership skills is because the turnaround process is not just about crisis stabilisation but also about putting in place a strategy, new processes and an organisation that will prevent the company slipping backwards into another crisis.

The ideal turnaround leader during crisis stabilisation is the rare breed of individual who is absolutely decisive and autocratic when necessary, yet has the ability to motivate and energise people to attain

|                                | Management | Leadership |
|--------------------------------|------------|------------|
| Before the turnaround begins   | x x        | x x        |
| New leadership                 | x          | x x x      |
| Crisis stabilisation           | x x x      | x x x      |
| Stakeholder management         | x          | x x x      |
| Strategic focus                | x x        | x x        |
| Critical process improvements  | x x x      | x          |
| Organisational change          | x          | x x x      |
| Financial restructuring        | x x        | x x x      |

| x       | Necessary |
|---------|-----------|
| x x     | Important |
| x x x   | Critical  |

**Figure 1.2**   Relative emphasis on leading vs managing.


their best under intense pressure. Such leaders have the focus and unwavering determination to see their organisation survive. They are fantastic communicators. They are aware of their own shortcomings and choose senior teams with skills that are complementary to their own. However, a consensus leadership style is required to convince stakeholders to support a turnaround in the first place and for financial restructuring. Fixing the business requires an authoritative but moderately autocratic style, while moving to sustainable recovery requires a complete shift towards a more affiliative and coaching style of leadership. Unfortunately most turnaround professionals lack the entire spectrum of leadership and management skills to do this. For a turnaround leader to take a business all the way through the turnaround process to sustainable recovery, he or she needs to demonstrate an extremely wide range of management and leadership capabilities, adopting the right approach and emphasis at the right time and in the right measure.

Providing they know their weaknesses, which appears to apply in most cases, then the necessary capabilities can be either brought into the top team or temporarily hired from outside sources. One of the most common areas where this occurs is in financial restructuring, where many turnaround executives do not have the necessary experience or specialised management knowledge.

## Goodbye Stereotype

Turnaround executives have often been characterised as tough, no-nonsense managers who "do not suffer fools gladly" and "do not take prisoners", and are often depicted as ruthless, autocratic individuals. Carlos Ghosn, who turned around Nissan and is now *also* CEO of Renault, was dubbed "Le Costcutter" and Al Dunlap, a US turnaround practitioner, was referred to as Al "chain saw" Dunlap. Jon Moulton of Alchemy, one of the more successful investors in distressed companies, talks of the need to be "brutal" or "violent" – by which he means being courageous in making tough decisions quickly, to remove or fix problem areas. While there is an aspect of successful turnarounds that usually requires deep cost-cutting and asset reduction, with the inevitable loss of jobs, this will only stabilise the business temporarily. Cost and asset reduction by themselves will buy breathing space but will never lead to a sustainable recovery situation. Most practitioners realise this and most acknowledge that they are not the right people to lead a turnaround beyond stabilisation and into subsequent growth.

Good turnaround leaders recognise that while they need to be autocratic to ensure that decisions are made and implemented rapidly – for survival – they also recognise that such a leadership style should be as short-lived as possible.

Many of the competencies that contribute to turnaround leaders' effectiveness in a crisis hinder them from being able to sustain leadership roles in the same organisation over the longer term. Their decisiveness and desire to control may breed caution among their subordinates. Furthermore, as they often lack patience they also lack the temperament to nurture new ideas. A few exceptional individuals can make the transition, but not many.

Individuals interviewed for our research all echoed the need to identify reliable, capable people, to build teams, to make managers accountable and to delegate decision making as quickly as possible. However, they also recognised the need to maintain tight controls during the transition phase until they could trust their managers to deliver the necessary results. Companies in trouble are often ill-disciplined, and lack any sense of a performance-oriented culture, so delegation without control is totally inappropriate.

We see two reasons why turnaround professionals have begun to pay more attention to people management. First, and probably most important, business managers are generally better educated and are not prepared to work in an autocratic environment – at least not for any length of time. Many turnaround situations today are in knowledge-based industries where the departure of key staff can make a turnaround extremely difficult to achieve. The turnaround leader must therefore get buy-in to the need for a turnaround and involve the staff to ensure that the recovery strategy is executed swiftly. Second, turnaround management is growing and developing as a profession. Historically, in the UK, it evolved from the accountancy and insolvency professions. Until recently most turnaround executives were accountants by training and so, for many, turnarounds were synonymous with a work-out, with a role akin to that of a receiver or administrator, focusing on cash management, cost reduction and financial control. This bias is still evident, but there are now more practitioners who have had senior general management backgrounds and recognise the link between good people management and corporate performance. Nevertheless such individuals also need strong financial capabilities to effect a successful turnaround, or at the very least know they need to bring in such capabilities into their team.

## Our Findings and Conclusions

This book is first and foremost a review of how the best practitioners provide leadership in turnaround situations. From our research, we can draw a few general conclusions:

1   There is a wide spectrum of leadership styles among turnaround practitioners: they do not conform to a single stereotype and different leadership styles can achieve a successful outcome.

2   While there is no single successful style, some common characteristics and approaches are exhibited by turnaround executives when acting as chairman or CEO.

3   Turnaround leaders, like good leaders elsewhere, are passionate about winning.

4   Turnaround practitioners are sceptical by nature: over-confidence and over-optimism are traits you will not find in a successful turnaround leader.

5   While turnaround practitioners are all quite autocratic in the early phase of the turnaround process, most recognise that they need to start to build teams and delegate as early in the process as possible.

6   All good turnaround leaders are also good managers, interested in detail.

7   Practitioners vary from those who are very short-term "cash crisis leaders" to those who are capable of fixing the company's underlying problems and can lead the business into subsequent growth.

8   Only very few practitioners have the capabilities or desire to remain with a business after it has been stabilised.

9   A few practitioners prefer to provide quiet leadership from "behind the scenes" – for example, as a chairman – rather than adopt the more visible leadership style of a CEO. However, the majority are outstanding communicators and recognise this as one of the most critical aspects of their role.

We conclude that the best turnaround practitioners are "hands on" leaders – highly visible inside their organisation and capable of dealing with broader strategic issues while remaining focused on the operational detail. They are comfortable moving back and forth ("morphing") between leadership and management roles. The best are true transformational leaders who help stakeholders recognise the problems, articulate a vision of the desired end state and motivate managers and employees to do what needs to be done. The range of leadership styles exhibited by practitioners leads us to conclude that it is crucial that debtors and creditors choose turnaround practitioners who are "fit for purpose". While some practitioners may be broad enough to have chameleon-like capabilities, many are only suited to "what they know". At a minimum, turnaround leaders must have leadership qualities appropriate for achieving crisis stabilisation.

While turnaround management is a generic subject and the same principles apply across nearly all industries, the leadership challenges are likely to differ as much as the management challenges in different situations. As we will see in Chapter 4, the turnaround executive needs to exhibit the 3Cs – clarity, credibility and courage – to grab control of the situation. The better the fit between the turnaround executive and the leadership challenges, the easier this will be. For example in B2B technology-based firms, where a crisis can spiral out of control very quickly, persuading customers to stay with the firm is usually a critical short-term action for the turnaround leader. We saw this with Archie Norman at Energis, Michael Capellas at MCI and Mike Parton at Marconi – all of whom needed to be "up front" and inspire confidence.

We now turn to Chapter 2 which provides the underlying framework for this book, but those readers who are familiar with our earlier work may prefer to move straight into Chapter 3.

# 2

# The Turnaround Framework

A SUCCESSFUL TURNAROUND DEPENDS ON DEVELOPING AN appropriate turnaround prescription and effective implementation. The first point addresses "what" needs to be done and the second addresses "how" to do it. In our earlier book, *Corporate Turnaround*, we developed an approach for achieving a successful turnaround that consists of seven essential ingredients, and an implementation framework consisting of seven key workstreams. This chapter summarises those two frameworks, since the rest of this book looks at how turnaround professionals provide leadership at each point in the turnaround process.

## Seven Essential Ingredients

The recovery of a sick company depends on the implementation of an appropriate rescue plan or turnaround prescription. Characteristics of the appropriate remedy are that it must:

- address the fundamental problems;

- tackle the underlying causes (rather than the symptoms);

- be broad and deep enough in scope to resolve all the key issues.

One of the challenges for any turnaround leader is to ensure that the rescue is built on a robust plan. Plans that try to tackle every problem of a troubled company, no matter how big or small, will fail as limited resources are wasted on tackling "non-mission critical" issues. The key is to focus on tackling the life-threatening problems. A recovery strategy that is based on the symptoms rather than the underlying causes may make the patient feel better temporarily but any long-term recovery strategy must be based on sorting out the underlying causes of distress. Turnaround plans must be sufficiently broad and deep to ensure that all the mission-critical issues are addressed. Turnaround management involves radical rather than incremental change. Very sick companies have serious problems that can only be tackled through fundamental, holistic recovery plans.

In our experience, we have seldom encountered a turnaround plan that was too drastic. The chief danger to avoid is doing "too little too late".

A successful turnaround or recovery plan consists of seven essential ingredients:

1  Crisis stabilisation

2  New leadership

3  Stakeholder management

4  Strategic focus

5  Critical process improvements

6  Organisational change

7  Financial restructuring.

Successful turnaround situations are characterised by significant actions in each of the seven areas. Failure to address any one of these may endanger the successful outcome of the turnaround.

We put crisis stabilisation at the top of our list because it plays a critical role in any successful recovery situation. By securing a short-term future for the business the turnaround leader creates a window of opportunity within which he or she can develop and implement medium and long-term survival plans. Creating that short-term breathing space is an essential prerequisite for a successful turnaround, as is our second ingredient, new strong leadership.

The third ingredient addresses the critical role of stakeholders in the recovery process and the importance of reconciling their often conflicting needs and rebuilding their confidence. The next three elements recognise the integrative nature of a business. Successful organisations are based on developing a viable strategy, and then aligning and integrating it with effective business processes and an appropriate organisational structure. Our final ingredient, financial restructuring, addresses the prerequisite of establishing a sound financial base and appropriate funding for the recovery.

Each of these core areas of the turnaround plan is supported by a range of generic strategies that address the problems most usually encountered in each area. Our list of generic strategies is set out in Figure 2.1. Clearly it is not an exhaustive list since each situation has its own specific characteristics that require a tailored solution. Nevertheless, there are a number of actions that are sufficiently common to most situations that we consider them to be generic turnaround strategies.

## 1. Crisis Stabilisation

In most turnaround situations crisis stabilisation will have to commence immediately. Substantially under-performing companies typically suffer from a rapidly worsening cash position and a lack of management control. In many situations companies are in "free fall"; senior management are paralysed in the face of an apparently hopeless situation and, very shortly, the business faces the very real prospect of running out of cash. The turnaround leader or whoever has effective management authority at the time must move very rapidly to take control of the situation and commence aggressive cash management.

The objectives of crisis stabilisation are:

- to conserve cash in the short term and thereby provide a window of opportunity within which to develop a turnaround plan and agree a financial restructuring;

- to rebuild stakeholder confidence by demonstrating that senior management have taken control of the situation.

The approach requires very strong top-down control. The turnaround leader moves quickly to impose a very tight set of controls for the entire organisation. Devolved authority to spend money,

| Seven key ingredients | Generic turnaround strategies |
|---|---|
| 1. Crisis sabilisation | • Taking control<br>• Cash management<br>• Asset reduction<br>• Short term financing<br>• First step cost reduction |
| 2. New leadership | • Change of CEO<br>• Change of other senior management |
| 3. Stakeholder focus | • Communications |
| 4. Strategic focus | • Redefine core businesses<br>• Divestment and asset reduction<br>• Product-market refocusing<br>• Downsizing<br>• Outsourcing<br>• Investment |
| 5. Organisational change | • Structural changes<br>• Key people changes<br>• Improved communications<br>• Building commitment and capabilities<br>• New terms and conditions of employment |
| 6. Critical process improvements | • Improved sales and marketing<br>• Cost reduction<br>• Quality improvements<br>• Improved responsiveness<br>• Improved information and control systems |
| 7. Financial restructuring | • Refinancing<br>Asset Reduction |

**Figure 2.1**  Generic turnaround strategies.

incur credit, commit the business, etc, is removed. Short-term cash generation becomes the top priority.

A critical element is to rebuild predictability into the business and the generation of rolling short-term cash flow forecasts becomes an essential management objective. The process of forecasting the short-term cash position, communicating the information to the stakeholders on a regular basis, and subsequently *achieving* the forecasts is crucial if their confidence is to be rebuilt. Crisis stabilisation requires very robust leadership; in most cases the turnaround leader is forcing a radical mindset change on the organisation.

It is also essential to implement a series of cash-generation strategies. Working capital is reduced by liquidating surplus stock, improving debtor collection and stretching creditor payments. All capital expenditure, except the most essential, is put on hold. Sometimes there is an opportunity to increase short-term revenues by price increases or promotional events – but this is the exception rather than the rule.

## 2. New Leadership

*New Chief Executive*

Inadequate senior management is frequently cited as the single most important cause of corporate decline, and therefore many, but not all, turnaround situations require a new Chief Executive Officer (CEO). Many investors and turnaround practitioners argue that in almost every case a change of CEO is required for two reasons. First, since the CEO was the principal architect of the failure it is very unlikely that he or she can form part of the solution. Second, a change of CEO has enormous symbolic importance; it sends a strong message to all stakeholders that something positive is being done to improve the firm's performance.

An alternative view, however, is that the immediate removal of a CEO may not be in the best interests of the company. It is a decision that may make stakeholders feel positive in the short term but one that they may come to regret at their leisure. It is important to remember that many CEOs of troubled companies have a strong track record of prior success; today's villain was yesterday's hero. Furthermore, the

CEO is often the person with the most knowledge and experience of the company and the industry-skills that may be vital to the company's recovery.

A second important consideration is the type of CEO to appoint to a turnaround situation. The basic choice is between a candidate with substantial industry expertise but no prior turnaround experience or the converse, an experienced turnaround leader or company doctor. The appropriate choice will inevitably depend on the specific circumstances. On balance, however, for most situations we would tend to favour a candidate with previous turnaround experience rather than industry knowledge. A good turnaround leader is usually a highly effective general manager, and experience suggests that effective general managers can usually work across most industries, other than companies that are highly specialised.

A further consideration is whether one person can lead an organisation through the complete recovery process from crisis stabilisation to restructuring and on to corporate renewal. The manager who is good at taking control, generating cash, downsizing and cutting costs is often weak at developing and implementing viable market-lead strategies for the longer term.

The immediate task of the turnaround leader is to rebuild stakeholder confidence by re-establishing a sense of direction and purpose. The leader must move quickly to initiate the development of a rescue plan, and communicate it to stakeholders. Finally, the leadership must be seen to be taking action quickly; it is essential to achieve some "early wins".

*Other Senior Management Changes*

Apart from the change of CEO, many turnaround situations are characterised by other senior management changes. Again views vary enormously among experienced turnaround professionals. There are those who argue for wholesale change, irrespective of the competence and willingness to change of the incumbent management. Proponents argue that such action eliminates resistance to change, sends a strong message throughout the organisation, and is a necessary part of the shock therapy that troubled companies require. The opposing view is that, as far as possible, the new CEO should work with existing management, with the proviso that the individuals are sufficiently competent and show a willingness to change. Irrespective of which approach is taken, most turnaround leaders will introduce a new finance director because of the critical importance of strong financial management in a turnaround environment.

Turnaround leaders rarely have the luxury of working with a world-class management team and workforce. However, large scale management change is rarely an option in the early days because it is not easy to attract good managers to highly unstable situations. Consequently, one of the major leadership challenges for the turnaround leader is to deliver superior performance from a relatively weak team.

Notwithstanding the above point the organisation requires sufficient human resource for the challenge ahead. Embarking on a turnaround with a team that lacks the basic expertise and experience required is a foolhardy exercise. At the early stage the turnaround leader needs to conduct a rapid management skills audit. The objective is to establish where the "gaping holes" exist and consider ways of filling the skill gaps. At the very least most organisations require effective financial, operations and sales and marketing management.

### 3. Stakeholder Management

Troubled companies typically suffer from poor relationships with their key stakeholders. Stakeholders, comprising debt and equity providers, suppliers, customers, management and staff, regulators, etc., can normally be split between "mission critical" and less important. The power, influence and importance of stakeholders will vary according to each situation. In most cases some or all of the stakeholders will be aware of the distressed nature of the organisation and will be concerned primarily about their own risk exposure to a failure of the business. A history of poor trading, inadequate communications, unfulfilled promises from management, and unpleasant surprises, coupled with the risk of failure will have eroded their confidence in the business. The other key issue is that the stakeholders will have different objectives and priorities. If the company is going to be rescued, these differing agendas have to be reconciled and stakeholder confidence rebuilt.

The guiding principle is that the turnaround leader must start to rebuild stakeholder confidence through a process of open communications and the provision of reliable information. Predictability must be restored and unpleasant surprises avoided at all costs. The role requires both impartiality as regards facts but also a robust advocacy of the company's position. Success depends on persuading the stakeholders to recognise and accept the reality of the company's position and work co-operatively towards a solution to the actual problems of the business.

Gaining stakeholder support requires careful stakeholder management, and the first stage involves the clear unbiased communication of the company's true financial position to relevant stakeholders. Based on that, the turnaround leader can commence a preliminary assessment of-stakeholder positions, and identify at an early stage the level of support for a turnaround plan (compared to other options such as sale, insolvency etc). It may be necessary to reach a standstill agreement and negotiate ongoing support from the company's bankers during this period. During the early stages of the turnaround, there should be regular communication of the short-term cash and trading position, and the turnaround leader should seek the involvement of stakeholders in the development of turnaround plans. Finally, the stakeholders' formal approval and agreement to the company's detailed rescue plan should be obtained. Ongoing communication of the trading performance and progress of the recovery should occur during the implementation process.

## 4. Strategic Focus

Substantially under-performing companies generally face one or more serious strategic problems. Strategic issues are invariably "mission critical" because they impact the *raison d'être* of the business. Few organisations have a natural right to exist. Continued existence depends upon establishing a business that delivers a service or product in such a way that it generates a return on capital that exceeds its cost of capital. This requires a robust and viable strategy that incorporates a clear sense of purpose and direction, realistic long-term goals that are based on genuine commercial opportunity, viable plans for achieving those long-term goals and an ability to outperform competitors based on genuine competitive advantage. Our experience with troubled companies is that they very rarely have a robust and viable strategy. Typically, a formal strategy has not been clearly articulated and written down, resulting in confusion across the organisation. Any strategy that exists is usually based on long-term goals that are either unrealistic or lack commercial common sense. Alternatively, the business may not be well equipped to achieve its long-term goals, lacking the basic resources and capabilities required to develop any competitive advantage, and the key business objectives for a turnaround leader is to develop a recovery plan that tackles these generic problems.

All the basic principles of strategic planning apply in turnaround situations. The strategic problems faced by many troubled companies may be very serious, but are often not complex, and although the solutions tend to be simple in concept they are not so simple in their execution. The desired end state or vision for the business must be clearly understood across the organisation. That destination must be intrinsically attractive – that is, profitable and based on an underlying demand for that service or product. The business must be capable of delivering a range of services or products, taking into consideration the resources it has at its disposal (infrastructure, people, know-how, technology, etc.) and it must be able to do so more effectively and more efficiently than its competitors. The strategy must be written down and widely communicated throughout the organisation. It should incorporate a simple definition of the goals and objectives of the business, and should encompass the "what" and the "how" – that is, what products/services are we going to deliver and to whom, and how are we going to do it.

The choice of strategy must take into account the existing resources and capabilities of the organisation. To the extent that the recovery strategy depends upon skills and capabilities that the organisation lacks, the gap must be manageable. A focus on the key success factors for the strategy must be at the heart of the recovery plan, since they provide the parameters within which the entire recovery plan must be developed. The product/market mix provides the target or focus for the entire organisation; it defines what products/services will be sold to whom. The importance of clarity on this issue cannot be overstated. Establishing a viable product/market strategy must be based on identifying a genuine customer need.

In many cases the strategic analysis will have to be quick and dirty. In our experience it is better to be "80% right and act" than "100% right and have missed the opportunity". Despite being "quick and dirty" the approach must be bold and broad. The danger for any turnaround leader is to use the excuse of insufficient time and analysis to postpone major strategic change. However, a sense of balance is also required.

Below we set out a brief summary of the most common generic strategies used in recovery situations.

## Redefine the Business

This is the most fundamental form of strategic change. The long-term goals and objectives of the organisation are changed; the management mindset changes and the nature of the business is redefined. For example diversified multi-industry conglomerates become industry-specific focused businesses, vertically integrated companies split, and multi-process organisations restructure around a single core process.

## Divestment

A divestment strategy is often an integral part of Product/Market refocusing. As the firm cuts out product lines, customers or whole areas of business, assets are liquidated or divested. The focus here is the disposal of significant parts of the business (division or operating subsidiaries), rather than the liquidation of current assets or disposal of surplus plant and machinery that we consider to be part of crisis management.

## Growth via Acquisition

A somewhat surprising but quite common recovery strategy is growth via acquisition. This does not necessarily mean diversification into new Product/Market areas totally unrelated or only marginally related to the firm's existing business. It may mean the acquisition of firms in the same or related industries. Acquisitions are most commonly used to turn around stagnant firms; that is, firms not in a financial crisis but whose financial performance is poor. The objective of growing by acquisition rather than by organic growth is related to the faster speed at which turnaround can be achieved by following the acquisition route. It is a strategy available to few firms in a crisis situation because they lack the financial resources to make an acquisition although, once survival is assured, acquisition may be part of the strategy to achieve sustainable recovery.

## Product/Market Refocusing

Less radical than a complete redefinition of the business but still involving fundamental strategic change is a refocusing of the product/market mix. This occurs at the operating company or business unit level and involves the firm deciding what mix of products or services it should be selling to which customer segments. The distressed firm has usually lost focus by adding products and adding customers while continuing to compete in all its historical product or market segments, i.e. adopting a strategy of being "all things to all people". Pareto (80 : 20) analysis quickly shows that there is usually an excessively broad product range and broad customer base, much of which consists of loss-making or low-margin business. In the early stage of turnaround the appropriate product/market strategy usually involves exiting unprofitable products and customers and refocusing on those that are relatively more profitable.

## Outsource Processes

Outsourcing addresses the position of an organisation within the value chain of the enterprise system within which it operates. The rationale behind outsourcing is to focus on profitable processes where the company has a relative advantage and to outsource the remainder to third parties who can perform them more effectively. Outsourcing one or more businesses or functions is a core element of enterprise transformation. Traditionally, outsourcing has been applied to non-core support processes with a heavy emphasis on finance and information systems. Increasingly, however, it is being applied to core functions and processes as multi-process organisations restructure to focus on only one or two core processes. Outsourcing is equally relevant to turnaround situations and is one of the generic strategies available as part of a strategic change plan. The emphasis within a turnaround environment is usually the urgent need to replace or enhance a substantially ineffective process.

## 5. Critical Process Improvements

Substantially under-performing companies typically have serious problems with both their core and their support processes. These processes are often characterised by high cost, poor quality and lack of flexibility/responsiveness. The underlying causes of these problems vary. Many processes are poorly managed due to a lack of focus on cost, quality and time. Problems with the physical infrastructure, such as state of machine repair, outdated IT systems and an organisational structure that breaks natural links in processes can exacerbate problems.

The tools and techniques of mainstream business process re-engineering (BPR) substantially apply. However, it is important that the turnaround plan does not become a BPR project. Turnaround plans are broader and deeper than conventional BPR. The emphasis in turnaround situations is on "quick win" process re-engineering. Standalone BPR projects are typically characterised by a strong link with technology and improvements to management information systems (MIS). These projects tend to be large scale and long term, with the emphasis on process improvements through improved computer technology. In a turnaround environment the reverse tends to be true. The approach is "quick and dirty" with the objective of focusing attention on the core processes. Typically this will cover procurement, conversion, logistics and sales and marketing. The emphasis is on achieving a rapid quantum leap improvement in time, cost or quality without the need for major MIS improvements.

Business process improvements generally fall within the following dimensions:

- *Time improvements*: Typically the focus is to make the organisation more responsive and more flexible by reducing the time taken to bring a product to market or by reducing manufacturing lead times.

- *Cost improvements*: The approach is to simplify processes to reduce both the fixed and variable costs.

- *Quality improvements*: This is self-explanatory and is about reducing rework loops, systematically analysing the reasons for nonconformance and putting in place corrective actions to improve processes.

Generic strategies deployed across the various business processes can be summarised as improvements to demand generation processes, demand fulfilment processes and support processes.

## Demand Generation

Assuming that product/market refocusing decisions have been taken, improving the selling process and the effectiveness of the salesforce is a key area for process quick wins. Marketing mix improvements include brand management/repositioning, promotions and, particularly, pricing. New product development and improved customer responsiveness may also provide important improvement opportunities. Although this area tends to be more important in enterprise transformation rather than turnaround situations, increasing the innovation rate and improved product engineering can sometimes have a significant short-term benefit.

## Demand Fulfilment

Typically this is the core area for process improvements and will involve substantial cost reduction and improved effectiveness in procurement, manufacturing/conversion, logistics and after sales service. Simple procurement initiatives can reduce cost, working capital and inventory risk and improve quality and service. Gaining control of the shopfloor and improving efficiency may involve layout changes and introduction of new practices such as cellular manufacturing, JIT and Kanban principles.

## Support Systems

The introduction of a production planning function to balance the supply and demand side of a business is an important generic response to a very common business problem. Other improvements will be targeted at "head office functions" and will include the introduction of new performance measures, improvements to the management of the physical infrastructure, and the restructuring of the finance department to deliver timely, relevant and accurate information.

## 6. Organisational Change

People problems are usually among the most visible signs of a troubled company. Typical symptoms include a confused organisation structure, a paralysed middle management, resistance to change and demoralised staff. Staff turnover is probably high, the most able people have left and the remaining workforce lack key skills and capabilities. Dysfunctional behaviour, where employees fail to co-operate towards achieving the corporate objectives, may be encouraged by silo thinking, a rewards system not aligned with the strategy, and a culture of non-performance. Significant organisational change is therefore required.

### New Organisation Structure

Changing the organisation structure can be a powerful way of rapidly changing the operations of an ailing business. A revised structure that facilitates clear accountability and responsibility will make the implementation process more straightforward. The turnaround leader will be able to see clearly who in the organisation is delivering against the plan and who is not. Any revised organisation structure should emphasise an external market-facing perspective, remove unnecessary hierarchical levels and seek to breakdown "silo thinking". Structural change should, however, be kept to a minimum in the early stages of a turnaround, as it can very easily lead to unnecessary confusion as individuals learn new ways of working and build new relationships. Even if no structural change takes place the turnaround leader is usually well advised to re-clarify management roles to ensure that there is no misunderstanding about what is expected under the new "regime".

### Accountability and Performance Management

Failing companies are nearly always characterised by a non-performing culture where managers are never held accountable for results. When a turnaround leader arrives his or her focus is totally short term and results driven. This is often the biggest shock to incumbent managers, and the single most important lever to improve short-term organisational effectiveness. New leaders quickly introduce performance goals and measure performance against them – often on a weekly basis in the early stages of a turnaround.

## Terms and Conditions of Employment

We believe that an effective reward system can play a major role in tackling the people problems of a business. The entire organisation should be strongly incentivised to implement the recovery plan. It seems to us quite obvious that people who feel they have a stake in the business, and who are financially motivated to implement a recovery plan successfully, are more likely to give their best efforts than those who are not.

In recent years changing contracts of employment and Union agreements have also been used as effective mechanisms of organisational change.

## Focused Training

Effective implementation of some-short term strategies may require some rapid capability building among certain employees, particularly where new systems have to be introduced. Focused training in such "hot spot" areas can lead to dramatic short-term improvements.

## Improved Communications

By far and away the most noticeable change brought about by turnaround leaders, and often their biggest legacy from an organisational perspective, is improved communications throughout the organisation. Good leaders, as we saw in Chapter 1, are good and consistent communicators of simple messages. Most companies could have better internal communications, but in a turnaround situation a quantum leap is usually necessary. As the company has gone into decline, less and less information has been communicated, cynicism has increased and morale has declined. The turnaround leader and his top team have to develop external credibility very quickly if they are to harness the organisation's resources. They therefore have to decide what to communicate, how to communicate it, to whom and where. In doing this it is crucial that they all communicate the same message.

An early stage initiative for the turnaround leader is to motivate the whole workforce. The main priority is to prevent good people leaving and to start to mobilise the organisation for the challenge ahead. Particularly during the early stage of the recovery, the organisation will move through very turbulent times, and having a committed workforce is a key factor for success. Frequent and open communication is critical.

## 7. Financial Restructuring

Companies in need of a turnaround typically suffer from one or more of the following:

- Cash flow problems i.e. insufficient future funding or an inability to pay debts as and when they fall due.
- Excessive gearing (too much debt/too little equity).
- Inappropriate debt structure e.g. excessive short-term/on-demand borrowing and insufficient long-term debt.
- Balance sheet insolvency.

Irrespective of the health of the underlying business, if the operating cash flow cannot finance the debt and equity obligations, the company will remain fatally wounded. In these circumstances the only solution is a financial restructure.

The objectives of any financial restructure are to restore the business to solvency on both cash flow and balance sheet bases, to align the capital structure with the level of projected operating cash flow, and to ensure that sufficient funds in the form of existing and new money are available to finance the implementation of the turnaround plan.

A financial restructuring usually involves changing the existing capital structure and/or raising additional finance. Capital restructuring usually involves an agreement between the ailing firm and its creditors, usually the banks, to reschedule and sometimes convert interest and principal payments into other negotiable financial instruments. The raising of new funding may involve additional debt, typically from the existing lenders who may be persuaded that the best prospect of recovering their existing investment is via the provision of further investment. The provision of new equity from existing shareholders via a rights issue or from outside investors (vulture funds, etc.) frequently accompanies new bank lending.

## The Implementation Framework

The starting point for the implementation of the turnaround process is always a diagnostic review to establish the true position of the troubled company and to determine whether a turnaround is a viable option, as opposed to insolvency, immediate sale or liquidation.

Once the decision to proceed with a turnaround has been taken by the principal stakeholders, seven separate implementation processes – or, as we prefer to call them "workstreams" – have to be undertaken to ensure that the seven key ingredients are in place. Figure 2.2 illustrates how the seven workstreams are linked to the seven key ingredients.

The seven key workstreams have been identified as:

- *Crisis management:* Taking control of the distressed business and implementing aggressive cash management.

- *Selection of the turnaround team:* Appointment of a turnaround leader and selection of his or her direct reports.

- *Stakeholder management:* Rebuilding stakeholder confidence and reconciling their different interests within an overall recovery plan.

- *Development of the business plan:* The development of a detailed recovery plan for the business covering strategic, operational and organisational issues.

- *Implementation of the business plan:* The implementation of the detailed turnaround initiatives contained within the recovery plan.

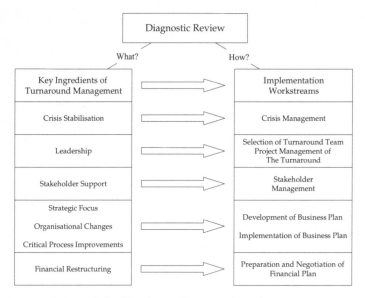

**Figure 2.2**   Key ingredients and workstreams.

- *Preparation and negotiation of the financial plan:* Restructuring the capital base and the raising of the money to fund the turnaround.

- *Project management:* The integration and co-ordination of the above six workstreams, i.e. overall management of the turnaround process.

Our experience is that in most turnaround situations the turnaround leader will have to undertake all seven workstreams, although financial restructuring may not be required where the troubled company is a subsidiary of a healthy parent. These workstreams are the essential implementation tasks of the turnaround process. Together the workstreams address the priority issues of managing the immediate crisis, fixing the operations, managing the various interests of those with a stake in the company, and ensuring that the company has sufficient cash to survive in both the short and the long term.

Clearly a diagnostic analysis phase must be commenced first because the turnaround leader cannot cure the patient unless he or she knows what is wrong. However, in many situations it will be crucial to commence other workstreams in parallel with the diagnosis, particularly, in stakeholder interface management and crisis management. One of the priority actions for the newly appointed turnaround leader is to advise the stakeholders of his or her appointment and explain how he or she intends to tackle the situation. On day one the discussion may be limited to an explanation of the process the leader he intends to follow. Such early initiatives start to rebuild confidence, demonstrate management control, and can help to prevent the stakeholders taking any adverse action prematurely. The other immediate priority is crisis management. The turnaround leader needs to rapidly assess whether the company has sufficient cash to survive in the short term, and while a diagnostic review is being conducted, he or she starts to formulate the recovery plan.

The analysis phase typically lasts between one week and three months, depending on the size and complexity of the problem. During the later stages of the analysis, the turnaround team will have already started to develop the detailed business plan. Our approach to business planning is intensive. The plan is "the bible" for the rescue: it sets out in detail the specific actions required to restore the business to profitability, together with associated trading projections. The process involves several interactions as each stakeholder inputs into the plan. How long this takes will depend on the size and complexity of the company but we would normally expect the plan to be fully developed within three to four months, and much more quickly in some cases. Even before the plan is finalised, implementation can commence. Many of the initiatives are "no brainers" and can be implemented before the plan has been fully and finally approved. The implementation phase typically lasts between six months and two years, and comprises an emergency phase, a strategic change phase and a growth phase. The financial restructuring is probably the last workstream to be undertaken. The key inputs for the financial restructuring are the operating cash flow forecast and funding projections for the business, and are usually contained within the business plan. As soon as these projections have been finalised, work can commence on restructuring the debt and equity and raising new money.

## 8. Diagnostic Review

In a turnaround process, the first task a prospective turnaround leader will want to commence is an analysis of the situation. Variously described as a strategic review, a diagnostic review, a business assessment, etc., this initial and critical phase has the following objectives:

- To establish the true position of the company from a strategic, operational and financial perspective.

- To assess the options available to the company and to determine whether it can be turned around.

- To determine whether the business can survive in the short term.

- To establish the stakeholders' position and their level of support for the various options.

- To make a preliminary assessment of the management team.

In many situations the troubled company may be rapidly running out of cash and the priority is therefore to move as quickly as possible through this phase. The approach is likely to be "quick and dirty"; analysis is high level, broad in scope, and in-depth only with respect to the key issues.

The diagnostic review needs to combine the elements of a conventional strategic and operational review with those of a corporate recovery/insolvency analysis. The team carrying out the review will therefore use traditional consultants' methodology: the strategic and operational review will cover both the internal and external environment with a view to establishing the causes of decline and possible recovery strategies. The financial review will focus on establishing the current financial position and future trading prospects.

The review will need to consider the various options available to the company – which are, typically, sale of part/all of the business, turnaround, insolvency or closure/liquidation – and evaluate the financial outcome for the stakeholders under each scenario.

The techniques for the review phase follow conventional consulting methodology, that is, analysis of financial and operational data, interviews with management and staff, tour of facilities, discussions with suppliers, customers and industry experts, and industry and competitor analysis.

At the end of the diagnostic phase the turnaround leader must have decided whether turnaround is a viable option, the outline shape of the turnaround plan (and the approximate level of funding to support it), preliminary management changes and the extent of stakeholder support. At this stage the turnaround leader may be either a turnaround adviser, a banker or a turnaround executive (as defined in Chapter 1).

At this early stage, it may not be apparent whether turnaround is a realistic option or not. However, within a relatively short period of time (a few days to a few weeks) the key stakeholders have to decide whether they wish to support a turnaround and, if so, who is to lead it – at least in the short term. If they decide to undertake a turnaround, them there are seven key workstreams to be implemented.

## 1. Crisis Management

As soon as the turnaround option has been decided for the distressed company, crisis management should commence forthwith – if necessary, even before a turnaround leader has been appointed. Where this is the case interim management or turnaround advisers can be brought in to deal with the crisis. The most likely cause of failure in the short term is that the business runs out of cash thereby preventing the wages, rent, etc., from being paid. The priority is therefore to establish the critical payments that have to be made in the short term to keep the company alive and determine whether the existing bank facilities, together with short-term cash receipts (such as debtor collections), will be sufficient to cover the critical payments. If the analysis indicates a funding shortfall, the turnaround leader must move rapidly to bridge the financial gap by arranging additional funding, pursuing aggressive cash realisation strategies and restructuring critical payments, wherever possible.

Simultaneously, the turnaround leader must move rapidly to take control of the organisation. The priority in the short term is to try to limit the scale of the continuing decline by focusing attention on the most serious and urgent problems. The key issue is to determine the factors, if any, that are an immediate threat to the survival of the business.

## 2. Selection of the Turnaround Team

Ideally an appropriate person will be appointed to lead the turnaround – usually a chief executive, but sometimes as chairman or Chief Restructuring Officer – as soon as the turnaround process is triggered by one or more of the stakeholders. This may or may not be before a diagnostic review has been undertaken. If the diagnostic review has been carried out by advisers or investigating accountants, their report is usually the trigger to appoint a turnaround leader and/or begin crisis management. Changing the top team may however take time: incumbents have to be assessed and where a replacement is necessary the recruitment process can take several months. Getting the right top team in place is usually a time-consuming task for the turnaround leader.

## 3. Stakeholder Management

We strongly believe that stakeholder management should commence at or even before the diagnostic phase begins. We will see in Chapter 3 how experienced turnaround leaders often commence stakeholder management prior to starting the diagnostic phase. The duration of the process varies considerably but our strong preference is towards a longer than a shorter duration. Experience suggests that debt and equity providers like to remain closely involved at least until the "patient" is almost fully recovered. In practice this is likely to be towards the end of the implementation phase, which can have a duration of up to two years, although this can sometimes be much longer, as in the case of Brent Walker, which went on for almost six years. One certainty is that the recovery path will not be smooth and uneventful. The company will probably experience continuing uncertainty and turbulence during much of the early recovery period, and it is much easier to retain the confidence of the stakeholders if they are kept fully informed of both positive and negative developments.

## 4. Development of the Business Plan

We believe that successful leaders of turnaround situations move very quickly to commence the development of a business plan which sets out their rescue strategy.

The conventional consulting model is followed. Problems are initially identified during the diagnostic review. Further analysis will identify the underlying cause(s) of the problem and from this one or more than one remedy is developed. Clearly there is a natural link between the diagnostic review and plan development workstream. In our experience the two have a "paralinear" relationship, i.e. they are partly sequential and partly parallel processes. Obviously, recovery strategies cannot be developed until the problem has been satisfactorily diagnosed; however, turnaround initiatives for problems that have been rapidly diagnosed can be developed while analysis continues on other more complex issues.

We strongly believe in the development of a comprehensive business plan. The plan should clearly state the long-term goals for the business together with the chosen strategy for achieving those goals. The plan should clearly define the products or services offered by the company, together with its chosen markets. The core business processes for delivering those products/services must be explicitly defined and the plan should contain a detailed programme of turnaround initiatives that together form the rescue process. Each turnaround initiative should be described in terms of responsibility, proposed action, implementation timetable, required resources, and proposed impact.

The number of initiatives varies according to the size and complexity of the organisation. The size and scope of each initiative may also vary from a major restructuring improvement (such as rationalising 10 factories to 4) to a more modest action such as the hiring of a new design director. Clearly the larger initiatives may comprise a major project on a standalone basis and thus involve a number of sub-tasks. In our experience turnaround plans usually comprise 50 or more recovery initiatives.

Finally, the plan should contain detailed financial projections for the first year and higher level projections over a three- to five-year period. The plan forms the 'bible' for the implementation process over the next six to 18 months. By the time the plan is endorsed, all the executives who are to play a part in its implementation must understand it and their roles. Managing the implementation of the plan becomes the key focus for the senior management.

## 5. Implementation of the Business Plan

The focus during this phase is the implementation of the turnaround initiatives incorporated in the business plan. The implementation of the business plan becomes the principal role of senior management. Although it may appear simplistic, it is generally the case that if an issue has not been addressed in the business plan, it should not be an issue for management during the implementation phase.

We believe that rigorous project management is the key success factor for implementation. The plan sets out a programme of prioritised actions with timing, responsibility, and planned impact. The implementation process employs conventional project management tools (Gantt charts, progress reports, etc.) to drive accountability; the priority is to get people/teams to deliver their initiatives on time and on budget. The progress of the plan must be monitored on a weekly basis, key issues must be dealt with when they arise and ensuing actions must be continuously identified. "Action" becomes the defining watchword for the implementation phase.

Management of the implementation process is driven by regular progress meetings supported by continuously updated rolling implementation reports. Ordinarily the co-ordination or steering group will meet on a weekly basis during the early stages; as the turnaround progresses the frequency of these meetings may to reduced to fortnightly or monthly. The focus for the meetings is the review of progress against each initiative.

## 6. Preparation and Negotiation of the Financial Plan

The business plan is the basis of the financial restructuring plan – if that is necessary. The financial projections accompanying the business plan will be from the basis of the cash flow forecasts, which form the key input into assessing the future funding requirements of the business.

## 7. Project Management

We have already mentioned the need for detailed project management of the implementation initiatives. However, the whole turnaround process needs to be project managed by the turnaround leader. He or she needs to fit the various parts of the turnaround jigsaw together, and must be able to mesh the seven key ingredients together at different stages of the turnaround process.

The turnaround leader does not therefore have the luxury, enjoyed by many other participants in the turnaround, of being able to concentrate solely on one key ingredient of the turnaround at a time. This is a difficult challenge for the turnaround leader as the objectives of each ingredient can be quite different. For example, the mindset and style required for crisis management are quite different from those required in business planning, yet these phases of the turnaround are managed in parallel.

# Timing

The turnaround process is characterised by considerable overlap of the planning and implementation phases. We identify four distinct but overlapping phases in the implementation process:

- the analysis phase
- the emergency phase
- the strategic change phase
- growth and renewal (beyond turnaround).

Figure 3.3 illustrates how the workstreams discussed in the previous sections are phased throughout the turnaround process.

## Analysis Phase

This phase encompasses more than just the diagnostic review. We have already stated that stakeholder interface management and crisis management often need to begin in parallel with the diagnostic review, and that the diagnostic review itself is the starting point for the development of the business plan. Thus we may begin to see some generic strategies – such as cash management, change of chief executive, tighter financial control – starting to be implemented in the analysis phase.

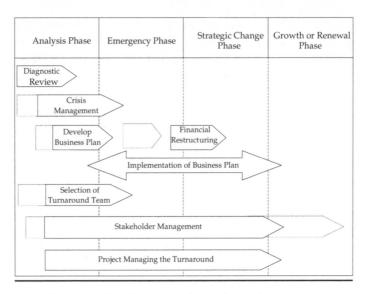

**Figure 2.3**    Phasing of workstreams throughout the turnaround process.

## Emergency Phase

The emergency phase consists of those actions necessary to ensure survival and therefore tends to focus on those generic strategies that can most easily be implemented in the short term. The distinction between implementation of the business plan and crisis management can become blurred. Thus, one finds cash generation, cost reduction, increased prices and increased selling effort as the principal generic strategies used in this phase of recovery. Organisational change to facilitate control and management may also take place.

The emergency phase is often characterised by surgery: divesting subsidiaries, closing plants, making employees redundant, firing incompetent managers, reducing surplus inventories, selling obsolete inventories, eliminating unprofitable product lines, etc. – all of which are designed primarily to improve the cash outflow and stop the losses.

It is during the emergency phase that the firm may seek additional financing to implement its recovery strategy and there is therefore an overlap with the financial restructuring workstream. The emergency phase will, typically, last from six months to one year, but may be longer if appropriate recovery strategies are not adopted or are not well implemented.

### Strategic Change Phase

Whereas the emergency phase tends to emphasise operational factors, the strategic change phase emphasises product/market reorientation. By good implementation of an appropriate recovery strategy in the emergency phase, the firm has assured its short-term survival and can begin in the emergency phase to focus strategy on those productmarket segments in which the firm has most competitive advantage (usually, but not always, those segments in which it is profitable). However, product/market change usually takes time to implement and may require some investment, which may not be possible in the early phase of recovery. It is at this strategic change phase that management and/or shareholders may realise that the long-term viability of the firm looks doubtful, or that the investment of money and time required to achieve sustainable recovery is not worth the risks involved. They may, therefore, decide to look for a suitable purchaser for the business.

Assuming that productmarket reorientation appears viable, the strategic change phase is also characterised by:

- An increased emphasis on profits in addition to the early emphasis on cash flow. Return on capital employed is still unlikely to be satisfactory at this phase, although losses have been eliminated.

- Continued improvements in operational efficiency.

- Organisation building – which may be important, bearing in mind that the organisation may have been traumatised in the emergency phase.

One US writer refers to this phase as one of stabilisation, because the organisation needs time to settle down and prepare for a phase of renewed growth. New management will probably have brought with it a new organisational culture which will take time to become institutionalised. Stabilisation is important, but alone it is insufficient to give the firm a sound base for the future. That can only be accomplished by refocusing the firm's productmarket position or sharpening its existing competitive advantages.

*Growth Phase*

Before this can begin, the firm's balance sheet must have improved. Once it has, the firm can start to grow, either organically through new product development and market developments, or via acquisition or both. This is the final phase of the turnaround process and the beginning of what is sometimes called corporate renewal. However, in some industry sectors, such as high technology, a rapid return to growth may be a prerequisite for a successful turnaround.

## Characteristics of Successful Recovery Situations

There are substantial differences between the recovery strategies adopted by successful turnaround leaders and those that are not. Successful recovery situations are characterised by:

- *A rescue plan that incorporates the seven essential ingredients.* A very common source of failure is to initiate too narrow a turnaround. The turnaround leader has to not only manage the immediate crisis and tackle the strategic and operational problems of the business, but also to rebuild stakeholder confidence and ensure that the company has adequate funding for the future.

- *An approach that addresses the key issues simultaneously rather than in a linear sequence.* In the early days, the turnaround leader should start the process of rebuilding stakeholder support in parallel with the early stages of managing the crisis and developing the business plan.

- *A rescue plan that is broad in scope.* That is, the plan should tackle cost reduction and revenue growth, deal with hard and soft issues, incorporate strategic and operational initiatives and address both short-and long-term priorities.

A study comparing successful and unsuccessful turnaround efforts undertaken by one of the authors in the UK and the USA showed that successful turnarounds are characterised by:

- management changes, particularly the appointment of a new chief executive and a new financial director;

- the use of multiple cash-generating strategies;

- improved financial control systems that are really used by management to install a performance-oriented culture;

- an understanding that cost reduction strategies, although important, may be insufficient to effect a successful turnaround;

- fundamental product market reorientation alongside improved operational marketing;

- significant organisational change in terms of structure processes and improved communications.

Two key messages stand out in examining successful turnarounds. First, successful firms use twice as many generic turnaround strategies as unsuccessful firms: they undertake a number of generic strategies in parallel. Second, they implement strategies more vigorously. There is nearly always a need for more action rather than less. We see this in practice when the initial turnaround leader is replaced because he or she is failing to make a real financial impact within the first 12 months. The replacement turnaround leader will always use more strategies and implement those of his or her predecessor more vigorously.

This chapter has summarised the seven key ingredients necessary for a successful corporate turnaround and what this means in terms of implementation. Further details of each of the seven key ingredients can be found in our earlier book, *Corporate Turnaround*. The remainder of this book will look at how turnaround executives provide leadership throughout the turnaround process.

# 3

# Before the Turnaround Begins

THERE ARE THREE CRITICAL STEPS THAT HAVE TO BE TAKEN before a turnaround can begin:

- Someone, or often a small group of individuals, must *initiate* the process.

- A *diagnostic review* has to be undertaken to determine if a turnaround is a viable option for the distressed firm.

- The key financial stakeholders have to be convinced to *support* a turnaround.

These steps are usually led by the key financial stakeholders – either the debtors (the shareholders and/or the management) or the creditors (the banks, bond holders and other credit suppliers). They, in turn, are likely to bring in advisers – accountants, lawyers, investment bankers, consultants, restructuring experts and company doctors – to assist in the process.

This chapter explores each of these steps and the nature of the leadership task from the perspective of the major players. All the players have the potential to participate in a leadership role that can affect the success of the turnaround process. As a general guide, where there is no equity interest left, the process will be led by the creditors otherwise the management or debtors keep the initiative and lead the process. In a recent case in which one of the authors was involved, management led the turnaround process even though the equity was lost, since existing equity providers were prepared to provide additional funding as a critical first step.

# Initiating the Turnaround Process

Some individual or group of individuals has to trigger the turnaround process, and this in itself may require considerable leadership skills. These individuals are normally financial stakeholders in the business or their representatives. In some situations the "writing will have been on the wall" for some time and the stakeholders are either waiting for the right opportunity to trigger change or they reach a point where they no longer believe that the incumbent management can deliver the required financial performance. In other situations a crisis will arise unexpectedly, and the stakeholders may only become aware of the problem when the company cannot meet its debt repayments, is in breach of its banking covenants, has a black hole in its accounts, or the reputation of the firm suffers a massive blow (as occurred at Andersens, for example).

Ideally the deteriorating financial situation will be picked up by the equity owners through their knowledge of the business and the expertise of the directors they have elected to the board. However, it is often the creditor banks, bondholders and other creditors who trigger the turnaround process because management (and the owners) fail to realise the gravity of the company's situation, or are just in plain denial. We will therefore start this chapter by looking at the leadership role in both debtor-led and creditor-led turnarounds.

## Debtor-Led Turnarounds

In publicly – quoted companies, it is usually a coalition of directors, often non-executive but not exclusively so, who lose confidence in the current leadership of the chief executive. They trigger the turnaround process by firing the CEO or by first initiating a strategic review of the business by outside consultants/advisers, which eventually leads to a new chief executive and a new strategy. In boardrooms, where there are a relatively large number of executive directors (as is often the case in the UK), and many of the non-executive directors owe their positions to their relationships with the chairman or CEO, it can be very difficult for an individual director or even a small group of directors to "take on" the incumbent chief executive, particularly if many of the directors feel they ought to be, or need to be, loyal – for whatever reason. A power struggle can easily arise unless the director(s) advocating change can gain the support of the Board and/or shareholders, as occurred at Marconi in 2002. If they fail to win the day – even if they are correct in their diagnosis of corporate distress and the need for a turnaround – the director(s) concerned are likely to be marginalised by the majority, and their best option is to resign. A public resignation is likely to have maximum impact on shareholders, and can be a powerful leadership statement about the need for change.

Fund managers are increasingly taking a leadership role in triggering change when they lose confidence in the management of a company in which they are significant shareholders. They often work behind the scenes putting pressure on non-executive directors to remove incumbent management, but there have been a number of instances recently where some fund managers have publicly raised their concerns about management.

Historically, debtor-led turnarounds of public companies have occurred as the result of under-performing companies being acquired either by more aggressive competitors in their own industry or by acquisitive conglomerates, and then being turned around. In the 1980s there were a number of UK companies such as Hanson Trust and Williams Holdings, that followed such strategies – although in the 1990s this type of activity was largely taken over by the private equity houses (the larger of which are increasingly looking like the conglomerates of the 1980s!).

In companies controlled by private equity houses, we see many examples of shareholders taking extremely active leadership roles both to trigger change and, in some cases, to manage the turnaround process. The process is helped by the shareholders' access to management information and their direct control over management and often the Board. The more "hands-off" private equity houses may bring in third party advisers to undertake a business review and/or change the chief executive, while some of the more "hands-on" houses will do the business review themselves and become actively involved in fixing the problems. Private equity firms that have invested in turnaround situations, such as Alchemy Partners, are nearly always in the "hands-on" category. The trigger for change is usually under-performance against budget or loss of confidence in the management. The firm might not actually be in a cash crisis, but the combination of the private equity house's control and its desire for quick value realisation triggers the turnaround process.

For example, in the case of Target Express, a parcel delivery business, the venture capital group 3i bought a stake in early 2000. At that time operating profits were £18 million on sales of around £200 million. In September 2001 it became clear that operating profits for the year were going to be only £14 million against a budget of £21 million. The company was also in breach of its banking covenants and would not be able to meet forthcoming principal repayments. This was the trigger for one of 3i's investment directors, Stephen Keating, to become actively involved in the turnaround of the company (see Box 3.2).

In an ideal world debtor-led turnarounds would be the norm since management and shareholders would pick up any signals of corporate distress very quickly and act upon them to avoid a financial crisis. In practice, however, the leadership action required to initiate a turnaround is often left to the creditors. For debtors to initiate a turnaround, existing management has to accept blame or, at the very least, to admit that there is a serious problem. In most companies, management, and the chief executive in particular, wield a considerable amount of power, either directly as in owner-managed businesses or indirectly in public companies where there is no dominant shareholder and often rather poor corporate governance procedures. The power of management to "do their own thing" and believe their own hype has been well documented in the recent scandals at Enron, Parmalat, Tyco and MCI.

Improved corporate governance measures ought to increase the number of debtor-led turnarounds, but it will depend on the leadership skills and, most importantly, the courage of non-executive directors to challenge management. Nevertheless, the vast majority of small and mid-size firms that get into trouble are likely to be creditor-led turnaround situations.

Creditors can and do play a supporting role in debtor-led turnarounds by aligning with the debtors who recognise the need for change and exercising their powers accordingly.

## Creditor-Led Turnarounds

Creditor-led turnarounds are more often than not initiated by the banks, although bondholders, credit guarantee companies, asset-backed financiers and even unsecured trade creditors can play a role in starting the turnaround process. The major banks all have credit assessment systems (usually using a 1–10 scale) whereby loans are regularly assessed. When the larger loans – limits vary by bank but are usually somewhere between £1 million and £4 million – slip from, say, a "5" ranking where some bad debt provision may already have been taken to a "6", the loan is transferred to a special corporate department dealing with corporate rescue.

The UK clearing banks have non-threatening names for these departments, such as Business Support Services at Barclays and Lloyds TSB, Special Lending Services at Royal Bank of Scotland, and Loan Management at HSBC. US banks are normally more direct and refer to them as "Corporate Rescue" or "Work Out" departments.

Client-relationship managers and senior divisional credit managers may sometimes have taken the initiative to persuade management about the need for change, but this is either ignored or insufficient action is taken. Bankers are usually loathe to become too involved for fear of acting as shadow directors. Furthermore, these managers deal with large portfolios of corporate clients – usually over 100 at a time – and have neither the time, the detailed knowledge of the company, the capability nor the incentive to become involved in a turnaround process. For bank management the key to success in minimising bad debt is to identify problems early enough and transfer the account to the internal departments who have the necessary expertise in corporate turnarounds.

Once management responsibility for the bad debt reaches the corporate rescue department, the banker will typically take an active leadership role in kick-starting the turnaround process. This involves three issues:

- Making the management realise just how serious the situation is, through clear communications ("straight talking") and/or putting pressure on the chairman or non-executive directors to take urgent action. Straight talking often requires no more than informing the company of its obligations under loan documentation, and indicating that the creditors will exercise their rights unless a turnaround begins immediately.

- Initiating a detailed diagnostic review which is either carried out by the bank's staff, independent advisers (often from the corporate recovery departments of the accountancy firms) or some combination of the two – for which the company is forced to pay.

- Initiating a meeting of all the principal financial stakeholders with or without the presence of management (although they will usually be invited).

On occasions banks will decide to kick-start the process by announcing without warning that the company's borrowing limit has been reduced. This can happen when a company is working within an agreed overdraft limit and receives a big cash inflow. The bank credits the account and reduces the overdraft by the amount of the credit! Such action on the part of a bank is only used if the bank feels that management is refusing to listen or act responsibly, and that the perceived risk of default is high. Any new borrowing is then made available on terms that trigger the turnaround. Unless it is carefully applied, the sudden reduction of overdraft limits can trigger insolvency instead of a turnaround!

The way the major banks deal with crisis situations in their portfolios depends partly on the leadership style of the senior executive responsible for the "recovery unit". However, Kendall Taylor of Lloyds TSB's view of his role is fairly typical:

> "I'm a stakeholder – rather than an adviser or practitioner – and I think the importance of this role varies from business to business, depending on how the funding is split and whether it is a quoted company. I am a stakeholder who at times becomes the pivotal stakeholder. I try to manage the business relationship with other financial stakeholders and the board of the company, to try and find a solution that trims the business back in the right direction."

Besides the obvious need for good "straight talking" communication skills, there are two key leadership characteristics are needed by bankers at this stage.

- *Courage to make quick decisions.* A number of senior bankers stressed that while they all have approval processes, given the nature of turnaround situations, they sometimes have to take quick decisions that are outside their "theoretical" authority. They take advice but as one said:

  > *"When push comes to shove I use my own judgement to do it, I accept that I won't get all of them right, but I wouldn't be here if I couldn't do it. It's what I'm paid for – to make decisions."*

- *Relationship building.* The sooner the bankers can build a relationship with management and other critical stakeholders, the more chance there is of avoiding insolvency. Building relationships with management teams, and owner managers in particular, can be extremely difficult because as one banker said: *"Denial still runs rife in our customer base . . . it is still the biggest impediment in kicking off the turnaround process."* The later the rescue unit becomes involved the more difficult it is. Kendall Taylor commented as follows:

  > *"Customers don't say 'I'd love to go to business support', so one of the key things is trying to establish a rapport with a customer when he is very concerned, even if maybe he doesn't show it. There are different times when we get involved and the nearer the business is to cash crisis the more difficult it is to establish a relationship. This is because for most businesses we deal with, while if we lent them more money it would take away the pressure, it would lose the bank more in the long run and in many businesses it would prevent them from realising the changes necessary."*

## The Diagnostic Review

The first substantial action once the process has been kick-started is to undertake a diagnostic review, which has six key objectives:

1   To assess whether the business can survive in the short term (a minimum of three months) or the extent to which additional funding is required to underwrite short-term survival.

2   To determine whether the company may be viable in the medium to long term.

*3*   To assess the options available to the company and identify those
     that offer the best value to the various stakeholders. These op-
     tions could include turnaround, immediate disposal, workout or
     formal insolvency.

*4*   To diagnose at a high level the key problems, whether these are
     primarily strategic, operational or both, and the mix of strate-
     gies and actions that are needed for short-term survival and
     beyond.

*5*   To assess the positions of the key stakeholders (lenders, share-
     holders, management, employees), their willingness to support
     and, if necessary, to help to fund a turnaround, their relative bar-
     gaining power and their ability to influence the outcome.

*6*   A preliminary assessment of management. Who is part of the
     problem? Who is part of the solution? Can we work with them?
     Should anyone be asked to leave immediately?

One turnaround adviser described the review process very simply:

> *"It is important to determine the situation the company is in, exactly
> how bad things are, how much time it has and what options exist for
> a rescue."*

The financial stakeholder(s) driving the diagnostic review have three
principal options:

- They can undertake the diagnosis themselves.

- They can bring in a third party advisory company to undertake
  the review. Historically the corporate recovery departments of the
  accountancy firms have been dominant in this area.

- They can bring in a turnaround executive or a specialist
  turnaround firm (such as AlixPartners) who they believe might
  be able to implement a turnaround if this option looks viable.

In theory, the process is relatively straightforward: gather data, process the data and make a recommendation about the best option for
the stakeholders. Of course this is not always easy because there is

very often a complete lack of reliable management information. Ian McIsaac of Deloittes sums up his approach as follows:

> "I find that all the answers are usually in somebody's head in the company, and not necessarily at senior management level. The key thing is to tap into the experiences and knowledge at all levels of the organisation. Using workshops and creating project teams is often quite useful. Time is the main constraint as decisions need to be made quickly and often on the basis of incomplete information. This requires a lot of **judgement**: anecdotes and facts need to be synthesised to yield good answers. At this stage, a true leader will use his personality to establish a relationship of trust and confidence."

Obtaining the views of individuals further down the organisation, at middle management levels and below is most important. Thus, at Lee Cooper, the apparel company (see later, Box 7.3) Paul Hick, the turnaround leader, found that the 65 people he spoke to below the directors had a very different story to tell from the reports provided by the nine directors during his first week in the company. Jon Moulton is also a fan of this approach:

> "In addition to hard analysis there are several simple ways to find out what is going on. Get an accounts clerk and relatively junior manager into the office – one at a time – and take 15 minutes asking about the problems. This will give you a pretty clear idea of what's going on . . . . Another thing I do is 'pull the string': simply chase an issue all the way through the company if it does not feel right."

Many advisers and turnaround leaders see the diagnostic review as essentially a classic management exercise requiring good analytical and technical skills allied to experience. Comments from advisers about this stage of the process support this view. Aidan Birkett of Deloittes described a recent assignment in the hotel industry:

> "I started by forming a team of people that understood the hotel industry both at the economic and operational levels. At the micro level, I needed people who understood levels of discounting, room rates, and typical levels of occupancy. They began by working on models to understand the cash-generating capabilities of the company, what levels

*of debt it could serve and where the value lay within the business. Following extensive modelling and review, the team and I identified what options were available to raise cash to support the company in the short term . . . raising new equity, increasing the borrowings, divesting some of the company or even just putting it all into receivership. We needed to be very sure of what we could get from the company in terms of profits and cash, and how we could improve it given the existing business and assets. Once we had decided what option was best for the stakeholders, we prepared detailed plans and forecasts and submitted a recommendation. Above all else, after three weeks of the diagnostic phase, I wanted to know 'more than the existing management team'. The remainder of the team that I put together consisted of individuals with experience from within the hotel industry and an insolvency practitioner to understand the company's negotiating position. We calculated what each creditor stood to gain or lose under differing scenarios and outcomes.*

The initial diagnostic review usually has to take place quickly, particularly if the cash crisis is already acute. Indeed it is not unusual for a turnaround practitioner, particularly an adviser, to arrive at a company to undertake a diagnostic review only to find within hours of arrival that the wages cannot be paid at the end of the week, suppliers have already stopped supplying or key assets are about to be seized. In such a situation the crisis stabilisation phase must start immediately in parallel with the diagnostic review. Similarly, in the turnaround of an operating company within a larger group, a new CEO is often unable to begin a diagnosis until he or she has accepted the job. However our interviews with turnaround executives indicated that they all felt it important to undertake at least a one-day "quick and dirty" analysis, before accepting an assignment. A number of company doctors spent up to four weeks undertaking a detailed business analysis, including a fairly detailed review of the industry and the firm's strategic position within its industry, in addition to the normal financial and management review.

Very often the problems are obvious. David Hoare, an experienced turnaround executive, says:

*"Within the first few days of being inside an organisation the major issues should stand out without significant detailed analysis. . . . At*

*Virgin Express, the charter business, the inefficient route network and the second hub in Ireland stood out as different from the operating models of other low cost airlines."*

One adviser, specialising in the recovery of smaller companies, normally makes a conclusion by the end of the first day:

*"You need to make a decision by the end of the first day on whether the business is recoverable or not. The decision then forms the basis of the work you may need to conduct . . . such as preparing the business for sale, finding a buyer, allowing receivership to occur."*

At Liberty's Department Store in London, John Ball (Managing Director of Retail Operations) says:

*"Even without information one can work around the business and quickly notice what is out of order. . . . Liberty, for example, had five full warehouses supplying only one department store, providing a strong indication that the company was overstocked."*

While good analytical and technical skills are obviously important, it is our contention that the manner in which the diagnostic review is undertaken impacts both the quality of the review and the chances of a successful turnaround. A number of company doctors – more so than advisers – are extremely aware of this. In our interviews they stressed the importance of listening to employees and the way in which trust can be built during the diagnostic review. It leads not only to more and better information but can also make the early stages of crisis stabilisation easier for the turnaround leader.

One turnaround executive put it this way:

*"The availability of information is vital for the diagnostic review. Although analysis of financial data may provide a lot of valuable background data, to truly understand the root causes of the company's problems, it is vital to talk to the people in the business. . . . Your immediate task is to listen to the concerns and learn from the experience of as many staff members as possible. In the inevitable climate of fear and uncertainty that usually exists, winning the trust of employees*

*is extremely important. If a more aggressive approach is taken, it may actually have the opposite effect, making people suspicious and resentful . . . a more emotional approach may encourage staff to offer more information and analysis voluntarily. **When emotions are running high, to make progress, you have to work with them.***"

Another interviewee's approach and philosophy on undertaking a diagnostic review is also illuminating:

*"After looking at background information in a brief consultation with the management team, I form a preliminary hypothesis about the primary causes of the problem. I then question members of the board and senior management in more detail as to their concerns, perceptions . . . as well as eliciting their reaction to my preliminary hypothesis. I focus as much on what is not being said, knowing that managers can be defensive and unforthcoming in difficult situations. . . . I try not to be adversarial and to make incumbent executives see the problems for themselves. It's all about asking the right questions in the right way."*

Asking the right questions and interpreting the responses (based on one's experience) and then framing the problems correctly is what a good turnaround leader should do. Listening rather than talking is important during the diagnostic review to help to establish trust and credibility with the incumbent management. It is important not only how questions are asked in the diagnostic phase but also to "hear" what is *not* being said. Box 3.1 shows the outcome of the diagnostic review undertaken by Tom Driscoll and colleagues at a family-owned producer of private label soft drinks.

---

**Box 3.1    Crisis and Diagnostic Review at a Soft Drinks Company**

The company manufactured and bottled carbonated soft drinks, spring water and squash concentrate. Until 1995, the Group had a turnover of £63 million with £3 million profit. The carbonated drink division focused on low-cost, private label products. The bottled water division had a well-established brand name, with significant UK market share, and the squash (concentrate) division was one of only three major suppliers in the United Kingdom.

The Group was 100% family owned and operated. It had been in existence for over 40 years and had well-established, good relationships with its five major customers, the leading supermarket chains. While margins on the soft drink business were under pressure from increasing competition, margins from the bottled water and squash concentrate businesses were relatively healthy.

The company ran into operational and financial difficulties after a total relocation of its manufacturing facilities in 1996. The move from an old-established facility in Shropshire to large, modern facilities in Northampton was meant to provide the company with state of the art manufacturing facilities with greater capacity and closer proximity to its major customers. In order to pay for the expansion, the company increased its debt level from £4 million to over £35 million, leaving it highly geared. The initial plan was for this debt to be serviced from the proceeds of expanded production and lower costs.

Unfortunately, about the time of the move to the new facility, a new bout of intense price competition among supermarkets began, resulting in pressure on suppliers' margins. In addition, the company focused the development of much of its new production capacity on carbonated soft drinks exactly at the time when price competition became intense and drove down margins.

As of 1998, the Group was in severe financial distress. The company was unable to service its outstanding debts. Worse yet, this financial distress threatened to become operational distress: new facilities were running at only 25% efficiency, due to the failure to commission the new factory, combined with the lack of qualified workers who were not in place to run the facilities (old workers had been laid off prior to the move); and suppliers became concerned about extending trade credit. Over an 18-month period the company had gone from having little debt and high profitability to having dangerously high debt and losing money.

David James was called in by the banks to identify a solution, supported by John Darlington, and later Tom Driscoll.

*Diagnostic Review*

Before accepting the assignment, about four weeks of due diligence on the Group was undertaken. This included a study of the Group's finances, a study of the competitive environment and an overall industry analysis. Particular reference was paid to a consulting report commissioned by the banks to independently assess the viability and possible liquidation values of the Group. This report, by PricewaterhouseCoopers (PWC), identified a break-up value of £17–24 million.

Leadership at this stage of the process required independent thinking and judgement, and a willingness to put reputations on the line. Accepting the assignment and failing could make it more difficult to win additional projects in the future. This was particularly true as an immediate capital injection of £4 million was needed to keep the company in operation. The banks were very concerned about making an additional commitment and the family, although still involved, was also unable or unwilling to donate the necessary funds.

David James and his team concluded that the banks could get more of their cash back by continuing operations rather than by a quick sale and/or break up. The banks agreed to a turnaround but David James and his team only agreed to take the assignment if the additional £4 million were made available. The bank agreed to the funding on the basis that David James took executive control of the business and the family withdrew from the day-to-day running of the business. It was now September 1998. The new management team were keen to repay this additional funding as soon as possible.

See *Box 7.2 for further information about this turnaround.*

# Gaining Support for the Turnaround

Since turnaround is only one of the options available for dealing with a financially distressed company – the others are insolvency, immediate sale, etc. – there has to be an agreement (of sorts) among the key players before the turnaround can really begin. This is sometimes very hard to achieve and advisers or company doctors might have already started the crisis stabilisation phase of turnaround without the agreement of the key financial stakeholders. This is not ideal but not necessarily bad since some quick wins on cash management may convince wavering stakeholders that it is worth trying the turnaround solution.

Whether it is a debtor-led or a creditor-ed turnaround, the key financial stakeholders – usually the banks or investing institutions with the most to lose – have to agree a way forward. Financial stakeholders, company doctors and advisers all stress the importance of good leadership at this stage of the process.

Chapter 6 looks at stakeholder management in more detail throughout the whole turnaround process, and in particular the leadership role of the company doctor. He or she may indeed play an important role at this early stage in the turnaround process but often we find that it is the bankers, private equity houses and advisers who play key leadership roles in getting the agreement to follow the turnaround path. Target Express (Box 3.2) and a UK Telecoms company (Box 3.3) provide examples of good leadership in both debtor-led and creditor-led multi-banking situations.

---

### Box 3.2   Debtor Leadership at Target Express

*Background*

Target Express was acquired by 3i in a leveraged buy-out. Having performed strongly as one of the leading players in the business-to-business express delivery sector, it suffered a significant decline in profitability after taking on a major home delivery contract and allowing its costs to spiral.

*Review and Standstill*

The initial diagnostic review of Target Express, undertaken by Stephen Keating of 3i, the equity holders, concluded that the company had a viable business with genuine turnaround potential but was in deep financial distress. His review was very difficult due to lack of good financial control systems, but he concluded that it was worth while investing six months to determine whether 3i should give support to a turnaround process.

Stephen concluded that he could work with the CEO and that he would be capable of delivering the turnaround but he needed coaching and extra support. However, Stephen needed to be the person who focused on external relationships with the financial institutions. In particular he felt that he needed to manage the financial institutions' expectations, not only on what they had to do, but also on what it was possible to achieve. It was a fine balancing act.

In January 2002 Stephen managed to agree a standstill for six months with the mezzanine and senior lenders. The company serviced interest but did not make scheduled principal repayments. He knew he it would need more time but also knew that six months was the maximum the lenders would give him. His strategy was to go with the six months and make sure the company lived up to the lenders' expectations during that time. He thought that it would put him in a position to ask for more time after the initial six months standstill period. In June there would be something concrete to negotiate about; in January there wasn't from the lenders' perspective. This also gave him the six months he needed to determine if recovery was a genuine option.

*Relationship Building with the Management Team*

Stephen realised that the success of his task greatly depended on the management. He had to make sure that they were all in-volved in making the change happen, and that they understood the what, the why and the how. To achieve this shared understanding he first had to establish trust and build binding relationships with the management team.

Although the management team were 10–20 years older than Stephen, he gained their respect and built relationships with them by displaying his professionalism, commitment to their company and making sure they understood that they would benefit from his involvement. He earned credibility by asking pertinent questions, listening and reflecting: all the time slowly building trust.

Stephen had almost daily contact with them. He believed that the only way to get management on his side and together move the company forward was to build "robust relationships" with them. He positioned himself as a partner and a coach to the management. He found that open communication and being direct about the issues was the way to influence management effectively. He believed that making people understand why they need to do something was necessary to get them to respond. He needed to be demanding as to what he expected from management and he constantly found himself asking for more and more information. However, Stephen didn't always share his concerns with the management in order to keep them upbeat and to stop them panicking. He learned that the management team could be very emotional at this stage and he needed to take them through the issues rationally, "using both soft and hard words". He was supportive of them but also very clear about what had to be achieved by June in order to save the company.

During the initial six months the management were prone to being overly optimistic as to what could be achieved. Stephen knew that over-promising to the lenders in this situation would be fatal and he had to work closely with the management to ensure that they never promised anything they couldn't deliver. This was not a situation where they could afford to miss targets. If anything, they had to over-deliver to rebuild their credibility and be in a position to negotiate with the lenders when the standstill period was over.

Stephen found management very willing to change; however, there were some issues where he encountered tension. One of these issues was the subject of bonuses, when he told the management that they would not have their bonuses that year! He made management understand that it had to be done and in the long run it was in their best interests.

Stephen spent a lot of time coaching management on how to use internal financial controls to monitor the company's performance and how to effectively manage the relationships with the outside stakeholders.

## Dealing with the Financial Stakeholders

There were three important groups of external financial stakeholders: an equity syndicate, mezzanine financiers and senior lenders. Altogether there were 33 stakeholders in this group. Early in the process it became clear that the senior lenders (eight banks) did not believe that Target could be a successful turnaround. Stephen realised that talking to all eight would consume all his time and more, if he didn't design a simple process for communicating and negotiating with them. He used his influence to create a steering committee of the three most influential banks to drive things forward. He understood that it was important to demonstrate to other stakeholders that the most influential lenders were supportive of him. The committee had all the stakeholders' trust and was where the major discussions were held. Stephen also initiated a couple of meetings with all stakeholders present. He used those meetings as an opportunity to let management perform, and by taking a step back himself he was able to demonstrate 3i's support and endorsement of management.

Stephen described how frustrating his experience was when someone failed to co-operate. He tried all sort of ways of influencing his fellow stakeholders, even threatening to withdraw 3i's business with them! In the end he says the invaluable trait was to stay calm.

> ## Box 3.3   Creditor Leadership in UK Telecoms and Internet Service Company
>
> The first sign of financial distress came as a complete surprise to all the financial stakeholders as the company had refinanced and acquired a new loan only six weeks earlier. A five-member steering committee of bankers was formed to rescue the company, one of whom was George Arkle from one of the big US banks. Arkle advocated a creditor-led recovery instead of an immediate sale to a private equity firm, believing that the debt holders' recovery would be dismal in a market filled with disinterested buyers and opportunistic private equity firms.
>
> Initially Arkle's view was met with scepticism by other members of the steering committee. He did not have the power to force his views on the group but through clear analysis, persuasiveness and good communication skills he eventually won over their support. "*All I was able to do was to advocate a vision, propose a viable alternative and guide others to 'see the light',*" said Arkle. "*I had to read the situation and not push too hard, otherwise I would surely have failed.*"
>
> Once a creditor-led turnaround was agreed in principle, Arkle changed from a selling leadership style to a more participative style, working with the other steering committee members to identify a new management team. During this stage, Arkle succeeded in improving the creditors' bargaining power against the private equity firms by keeping all alternatives in play and balancing the needs of the different stakeholders. Today the company trades healthily and Arkle's role is that of a non-executive director.

Specialist restructuring firms and experienced company doctors stress the importance of obtaining stakeholder support, prior to accepting an assignment to turn a company around. They want full authority to make whatever changes they think are necessary and usually want to ensure that there is sufficient support to finance the crisis stabilisation phase of the turnaround.

David Hoare says that the effective use of power before one accepts the role of turnaround leader is critical in ensuring support from key stakeholders: "*The ability to say no thanks is very powerful.*" Thus at Virgin Express, where he was already a non-executive director, he ensured that Richard Branson had bought into his plan for shrinking the airline before taking the role of Executive Chairman. David even tries to ensure the support of major stakeholders before undertaking a diagnostic review. At Target Express he obtained full support from 3i, the shareholder, mezzanine player and the chairman before undertaking his review. He says that this made his investigation much easier.

Several turnaround executives also expressed the need to negotiate stakeholder financial support – when this is necessary – as a condition of accepting a turnaround assignment. Once the assignment has been accepted they feel they have less power. Not all company doctors operate in this way. Peter Giles, who has been a turnaround executive for over 25 years, stresses the need to take a risk and step into a situation when the real management issues are still unclear and stakeholder support is uncertain:

> "*Building the necessary support from the different (financial) stakeholder groups to the turnaround process requires strong persuasion and negotiation skills. This is a judgement call and requires a lot of courage as none of the stakeholders will provide their full support until they feel comfortable with the situation... often later in the process. In one situation I was involved with there were six banks with £160 million of exposure to a company with a valuable core business but underlying value of only £65 million. The banks could not agree how to proceed. Rather than demand a set of conditions... I was willing to take the risk and get the banks' agreement later in the process.*"

While most boards of directors of companies in trouble have, in effect, failed by not dealing with declining performance at an early enough stage, many company doctors and advisers stress the need to obtain Board approval for their appointment and their financial plan. One individual insists on the appointment being unanimously approved by the Board before he will accept an assignment. Another says he likes to be very clear about the authority levels when he goes into a situation. Where family-owned businesses are involved, the situation is often more challenging, and there may be no chance of a successful turnaround unless the turnaround leader (company doctor or adviser) "bangs heads together" and threatens insolvency. Box 3.4 provides one such example.

---

### Box 3.4   Dealing with a Feuding Family

Charles Richardson was approached by a major high street bank to help a local company in the ship maintenance industry. It was losing about £2 million on revenues of £8 million, and was seriously short of cash. The only reason the bank continued to support it was because of its key asset – a valuable piece of land. The Board consisted of 11 family members, spanning three generations, most of whom had not talked to each other for years and refused to sit across a table from one another.

When he arrived at the company Charles had to make a series of "short and blunt" talks to various family groups gathered in separate rooms. He told them if they did not get together within 10 minutes, he would leave and the bank would put the company into receivership. They agreed. At the Board meeting that followed, he explained the perilous state of the company – much to the astonishment of many – and said the bank would give them a final chance if they would get their act together. Charles was made managing director with specific power "to call the shots".

---

Before accepting an assignment, the turnaround executive will have to be convinced (as far as possible given the available information) that the situation is recoverable or, at a minimum, that the objectives set by the financial stakeholder(s) are achievable. In arriving at this decision, experienced turnaround executives will assess the value they believe they can add to the specific situation. Most are good at knowing their own strengths and weaknesses and will decline situations if they feel the "fit" between their skills and the needs of the situation is wrong.

The final issue, but by no means the least important from the perception of the turnaround leader, is the need to negotiate and agree the basis of his or her remuneration. In practice one finds there is a wide variation in the ways in which company doctors are remunerated for their work. In large public companies there is the normal package of salary, bonus against targets and share options to align the CEO or turnaround team with shareholders' interests. In smaller companies, company doctors usually work on the basis of a daily fee plus an incentive (cash and/or equity) linked to either profit improvement or debt recovery. Rewarding company doctors by giving them a percentage of debts recovered is common in creditor-led turnarounds, but can obviously lead to emphasis on a workout rather than a turnaround. Advisers tend to work on a per day consultancy basis although they are increasingly negotiating performance-based incentives. Aligning rewards with the interests of the stakeholders can be an important signal which engenders trust – a critical ingredient for the success of any turnaround.

# 4

# New Leadership

IN BOTH DEBTOR- AND CREDITOR-LED TURNAROUNDS, IT IS usual for a new leader to be appointed at the instigation of one or more major stakeholders. The new appointee may already have had considerable exposure to the company – for example, by conducting a diagnostic review in an advisory or consultancy capacity. In such cases, he or she will have conducted a preliminary assessment of management and will have identified the key problems and initial actions to be taken. In other situations, he or she may have had little more than a one-day "quick and dirty" analysis or even just a briefing and some limited financial information. In Chapter 3 we examined how the leader uses the diagnostic review process to evaluate the company and enlist the support of the key stakeholders before accepting an assignment. In this chapter and the next, we examine how the new leader takes control of the troubled company and begins the process of stabilisation and recovery.

The immediate challenges facing the new leader are:

- to become established as the "de facto" leader and take management control of the organisation;
- to put in place an appropriate senior management team to drive the turnaround;
- to establish a clear sense of urgency among the existing management and workforce.

There is relatively little time in which to accomplish these tasks when a company is in financial crisis. Therefore, from the moment they arrive, turnaround leaders must drive down the twin tracks of management and leadership, "morphing" between the two as necessary to achieve their purpose. They do not need or seek the affection of those they lead but must quickly gain their attention, support and respect if they are to succeed.

The arrival of the new leader is therefore a key moment in the turnaround process – a physical separation from the past and the tangible beginning of a new era. The words and actions of the new leader during the first few days in office will lay the foundation for his or her relationship with the company and show his or her ability to create a shared vision, common direction and sense of urgency.

On rare occasions the new turnaround leader may come from within the company, as Mike Parton did at Marconi. Interestingly these individuals, where they are successful, adopt a virtually identical approach to that of experienced company doctors (see Box 4.1 for Mike Parton's actions at Marconi).

---

**Box 4.1    Marconi: A New Leader from Within**

Marconi was one of the most complicated financial restructurings ever seen in the UK. From the first sign of trouble – a profits warning in July 2001 – to final court approval of two schemes of arrangement, the restructuring lasted almost two years and encompassed fundamental management, operational and financial changes including a Board clear-out, disposals of over 20 businesses, reducing headcount by over 50%, two separate schemes of arrangement and a stock market de-listing and re-listing. As the financial restructuring progressed, supported by armies of advisers, the management team was simultaneously leading a major operational turnaround to ensure the long-term viability of the stricken telecoms supplier.

In 1996, George Simpson took over as Managing Director of GEC, after Lord Weinstock had spent 33 years at the helm, building it into the undisputed leader of the British electrical industry. Under Simpson and his new management team, GEC pursued a strategy of focusing on communications and IT, which culminated in 1999 in the demerger of GEC's Electronic Systems business (which merged with British Aerospace), the debt-funded acquisition of two major US businesses (in telecoms and internet switching) and a change of name to Marconi plc. By mid-2001, it was apparent that the telecoms boom was slowing and that demand for Marconi's products would fall considerably short of expectations. Profit warnings followed and the share price collapsed from a peak of over £12 to below £1, as the markets worried about the company's debt mountain and continuing cash outflows due to operating losses. By September 2001, the chairman, chief executive and chief executive elect had all resigned and the company had commenced discussions with its lenders to restructure over £4 billion of debt.

A change of leadership was inevitable after Marconi's very public fall from grace. Unusually for a large-scale public company turnaround, the replacement CEO came from within the group in the person of Mike Parton, a divisional CEO. On taking control, Mike's first action was to establish a new 'cabinet' consisting of six key managers, each charged with overall responsibility for one of six key areas: customers, costs, strategy and planning, refinancing, asset disposals, and people and communications. He abandoned the group's complex matrix organisational structure and centralised control, managing through 12 senior managers in total including his "cabinet" of six and six key regional managers. In an important symbolic act, the "cabinet" was selected from across the group and Mike did not "import" his former divisional management team to fulfil these roles.

Mike describes his leadership style at this stage as a "trench warfare mindset". Like Mike, his senior managers had been with Marconi for some time and believed that their careers would be finished if they did not succeed in turning the business around. Failure was not an option and Mike adopted a dictatorial approach to ensure that everyone was focused on survival, through delivery against short-term imperatives. Mike described his job as to "focus on the things that will kill us", in particular ensuring there was sufficient cash to see the restructuring through.

Having established a high-level recovery plan with the "cabinet", Mike's key leadership task was to communicate with the rest of the management team, with employees, with customers and with the outside world. Marconi's distress, after years of stock market adulation, was attracting tremendous media interest, and it was vital that customers, suppliers and employees heard management's views rather than press speculation. Mike established a series of internal communication channels, including:

- weekly 1-hour call with the senior management team (top 50) to communicate and monitor progress on critical issues;
- quarterly off-site conference with the same top 50 managers, to establish short-term priorities;
- "town hall" meetings in each major office, enabling all employees to hear at first hand from the leadership and to question them directly;
- a website, "Ask Mike", where every employee could ask Mike questions directly;
- sending a fortnightly email ("Mike's view") to all employees, supported by regular voicemails and conference calls. These were always focused on the key priorities – cash and costs – reinforcing the many operational initiatives that were underway (see Box 5.1 in Chapter 5).

Mike's other major task, after communication, cash and costs, was to retain and motivate his senior managers through the tremendous challenges of the long restructuring operation. A series of redundancy programmes and disposals had reduced group headcount by over 50%, but it was vital to ensure that certain key managers remained. Mike implemented a retention plan for key individuals and subsequently rolled this into a senior management share option scheme, which took effect once the restructuring was completed.

Finally, Mike put himself on the line. The pay-offs to the former Marconi leaders had caused widespread outrage in the press. On his own initiative, Mike requested that the Board amend his contract so that there would be no pay-off if he were removed as CEO. Mike aligned his interests completely with his stakeholders; substantial rewards were available for success, but there was to be no "reward for failure" if the turnaround did not succeed.

# Making an Entrance

In the majority of cases, the new leader will replace the incumbent chief executive, or arrive as Executive Chairman. Turnaround practitioners recognise that their style, methods and above all their words will be subject to the closest scrutiny on arrival. Their personality will be inferred from their physical presence, style of dress, choice of car, mode of address, even the parking place they select or the office they choose. Experienced leaders do their homework in advance and are well prepared for day one, as indicated by the following quote:

*"The very first day, when you arrive, the people understand that it is the beginning of a new phase. I usually spend a lot of time preparing for the first day, as first impressions are critical. . . I choose my words very carefully."*

Thus, at the Royal Mail on the day after his appointment as chairman, Allan Leighton turned up at the Leeds sorting office for the early morning shift to talk to staff. Such actions send strong signals throughout organisations.

The approach of one turnaround leader is perhaps typical of what some might expect of a company doctor. He is conscious that his physical presence gives him a certain amount of gravitas. He consciously dresses in a black suit with a white shirt and there are no smiles. He arrives early in a big car (he drives a Mercedes 500) and if he feels that a symbolic gesture is needed, he sometimes rips out the reserved parking spaces near the entrance. It must be said that at around 6ft6 with a beard, he has an intimidating physique that helps him to convey the required image. He emphasises the need to grab people's attention. In most companies people are afraid of him when he arrives. In his own words: *"It's about putting the fear of God in them and then just sitting back and looking presidential."*

Styles certainly vary. One described his fellow turnaround professionals as ranging *"from practitioners who were physically threatening to those so smooth that you wouldn't feel the knife going in"*. Whatever their approach, turnaround leaders need the ability, from the earliest days of their appointment, to convince people to trust and follow them, to make them feel that *"you are their best chance to get there"* and to accept and eventually embrace the changes necessary for survival and recovery.

Staff in most troubled companies will be at least vaguely aware before the new leader arrives that all is not well. However, it is almost certain that they will not know just how bad the situation is, since incumbent management may not have realised it themselves and will often have been denying the difficulties and seeking to reassure staff with optimistic messages for some time beforehand. Therefore, the sudden change of leader is likely to come as a shock to some, if not most, employees.

## Taking Control

The leader's first task is to take control. In some situations, the mere fact of the new leader's arrival (particularly if the previous CEO has just been removed) can be enough to shock the organisation awake. The new leader must move swiftly to establish control. The initial point of contact is usually a meeting with the Board and/or the senior management team. If the CEO is still present, removing him may be the first priority. In extreme situations, the whole Board might be removed at the outset. As one turnaround executive described it:

> *"At the AGM, the Chairman asked how I would like to run the meeting. I became Chairman, took out [fired] the finance director, took out 6–7 other directors and was left with one, the company secretary."*

In another situation a company doctor arrived with undated resignation letters which he gave to all the Board, saying "nothing happens until you all sign these". By doing this he was getting them to accept that the crisis was their fault and that he was now in control.

The initial meeting may not always be quite that dramatic, but it should achieve three key objectives:

- To establish that the new turnaround leader is in charge; as evidenced by the removal of his predecessor and others if necessary.

- To communicate with absolute clarity the nature and extent of the problems, the absolute requirement for change and the new rules of engagement.

- To expose the attitudes (and to some extent the capabilities) of the remaining senior management.

The leader's style at this meeting is usually extremely autocratic and these can be highly charged occasions. The facts will be unpalatable: the causes and severity of the company's situation, the extent of the cash crisis and the limits to ongoing stakeholder support that should be assumed. Typically, under-performing companies have entered a downward spiral. Information is deliberately or subconsciously withheld as managers seek to avoid sharing or hearing bad news, and increasing isolation and secrecy result in blame or denial. Inappropriate actions are taken (or, more typically, insufficient or inadequate actions) and the decline accelerates. Therefore, it can come as a great shock even to senior management to hear the extent of the problems and be informed of the short distance that stands between survival and failure. Such a shock may be necessary to galvanise the remaining management into action:

> "You lay out very clearly the status of the organisation including the consequences of failure in order to have them understand the urgency of the situation."

> "You have to leave people in absolutely no doubt that there is a cliff, a precipice."

> "You have to shock the organisation awake. . . . You have to be prepared to ride roughshod over people to get the job done."

It is important to bear in mind the likely psychological state of the audience. Aidan Birkett of Deloittes describes it thus:

> "By this time, the management team have usually arrived in a situation that . . . they have lost their pride, they have no energy or they are out of their depth. People within the business often do not want to be disturbed from their slumbers, so sometimes you have to fire people, but you have to be fair and straight without any preconceived notions or prejudices. Sometimes the management are in a hole and they just

*have to stop digging. If they don't stop, you have to take the shovel
off them and hit them on the head with it."*

The turnaround leader has to maintain a fine balance between describing the problems in sufficient detail to convince his audience
and reciting a litany of failure that creates or perpetuates a culture
of blame and fear. It is likely that some or all of the architects of
the crisis will be present and are, in effect, being held to account.
Their responses are likely to be instinctive and defensive. One leader
summarised it in this way:

*"They don't like you, they resent you. No-one likes being told they
are a failure."*

The main leadership challenge is to take executive control and to
change senior management's mindset quickly towards crisis stabilisation and short-term survival. This means letting go of those who
will not or cannot actively buy into the turnaround process.

It is the leader's role to steer the management team away from blame
and counter-blame and towards taking the actions necessary to address the resulting crisis. However, this is not a time for soft words.
The message to management must be explicit and unequivocal; they
can acknowledge the problems, accept the new regime and work towards a solution or they must go:

*"If they stand in my way, I remove them, but I give them the option."*

The task of the turnaround leader is to deal routinely and unemo-
tionally with these highly stressed situations, remaining calm, confident and detached. At the same time, he or she must anticipate and
manage the turmoil of emotion around them, as described by one
experienced leader:

*"What is normal to me causes people to have heart attacks. Gen-
uinely [because of] where and how we operate, I have seen people
physically collapse from tension. One of my problems is not to lose
sight of that. Because what is to one person a show-stopping incom-
prehensible problem is to me just a step in the process so that I can
make it to the dinner party later tonight. There is a clear need to lead*

*with a clear and controlled process and not go too cold and too fast so that I leave a vacuum of the management team behind me. They [the management team] have already been through hell two or three times before and I can't forget that just because I've seen it and done it before . . . I must not forget to see it from their perspective."*

The initial meetings will set the tone for the new leader's relationship with his or her senior managers and may ultimately dictate the success or failure of the turnaround. As we will discuss in subsequent chapters, at certain phases of the turnaround a more consensual and consultative approach becomes necessary but at this initial stage coercive leadership is typically more appropriate. Nonetheless, the turnaround leader walks a tightrope between galvanising his or her audience and alienating them, stirring them to positive action or inciting fear, resentment and obstruction. Although leaders have the power to remove those in their way, they risk destroying the business if they drive too hard, too fast and are not seen to be objective.

*"It's a fool that goes in with the macho style and just blindly says 'do this, do that my way'. We put in a very tough finance director in a company and he very nearly trashed the company. He robbed people of their creativity and almost killed the company."*

Pippa Wicks at AlixPartners says:

*"Instead of firing somebody – take action quickly to solve something the previous leader was unable to do. Quick wins are important in a crisis because they help build the new leader's credibility."*

Many leaders make an early "easy" decision of a symbolic nature to demonstrate that "from now on things are going to be different". Sacrificing sacred cows, such as cancelling a major overseas trade exhibition that has become the annual outing for senior management, or killing a pet project of the former CEO, can send an immediate and powerful message to the organisation.

Patrick O'Sullivan who led the turnaround of Zurich Financial Services in the UK (see later, Box 9.2) says:

*"Never judge a book by its cover. Give yourself time to assess the strengths and weaknesses of your team. It is generally good if colleagues*

*say he or she is a tough performer provided they share your definition of tough performance."*

Experienced turnaround leaders know that their leadership style may not be appropriate in all circumstances. In professional services and some high tech firms, where there are high levels of intellectual capital, turnaround leaders still need to be firm but must to some degree respect individuals' professional values. This requires less telling and more listening and convincing as a style.

## Meeting the Team

Having "seized control" at the "top table", the next round of meetings address both a management objective – to get to the detailed information – and a leadership task-to establish a core team to drive the turnaround process. Many practitioners use a series of one-on-one meetings with senior managers to achieve this. Prioritising the people you want to talk to is important, and simple criteria are usually applied, such as focusing first on those who either generate or consume cash. These meetings serve multiple purposes:

- To assess the individual's capability and value to the turnaround process.

- To identify key influencers and use them to "spread the gospel".

- To draw out detailed information from those closest to the business and get all the problems on the table as quickly as possible.

- To establish the new way of thinking and operating, based on full disclosure and open communication.

- To clarify job responsibilities and reporting relationships.

Some practitioners recommend visiting people in their offices rather than "summoning" them; they find that managers are more confident and willing to "open up" on their own territory. They are also mindful of the symbolic message, particularly in a hitherto hierarchical or formal organisation, that the new leader "rolls up his sleeves and gets stuck in."

In our experience it is also vitally important for the new leader to clarify job responsibilities and reporting relationships. We find that complicated and confused management organisations are a common feature of larger companies in trouble, leading to poor or non-existent decision making. We often find companies – of all sizes – in which it is unclear who is responsible for even the most simple decisions. The problem can be compounded when a new leader arrives, as "everything stops" as managers and employees alike become insecure and unsure whether they can make any decisions at all! It is always worth clarifying roles and responsibilities in these early meetings with managers even if it is no more than confirming that they should continue to work in exactly the same way as before, until told otherwise.

If the new leader has not had the opportunity to conduct a diagnostic review prior to his appointment, these initial meetings can be critically important in getting access to reliable information. Experience demonstrates that managers in the so-called "marzipan layer", (unseen until you dig beneath the executive board "icing", yet contributes much of the substance and flavour) usually have a very good understanding of the issues. Time and time again we hear:

> *"Most of the time someone in the organisation has a solution . . . my job is to dig through the organisation and find these people."*

> *"Management get in the way of people trying to do a job. People actually want to do a job well."*

> *"I try to work with the team. I have to rely on them for my understanding of the business."*

An integral part of the leadership role is to know not only the questions to ask but also how to frame them and how to listen. Communications are usually broken in a distressed company environment; previous management having become less and less inclined to solicit the truth or explain their actions, making them increasingly remote from the real problems. Simply listening while allowing employees to talk not only provides valuable insight into the business but also allows them to relieve the stress built up in an organisation in turmoil. As two experienced professionals describe it:

> *"You are not being judgemental – you are trying to coax them to communicate with you, displaying the body language of a kindly old*

*professor. I make sure that John (my numbers guy) keeps his bloody mouth shut. He not only sounds like a pompous git, he is a pompous git!"*

*"Build trust in them first to open the team up. Act as a listener and use body language that does not imply blame, simply that you want to learn."*

There is never enough time in a crisis and the tendency can be to rush through these early communications and "get on with the job". Experience suggests that it is important not to short-cut this critical leadership task. A prominent and experienced turnaround executive emphasised this point to us:

*"The place I stayed and stayed until I was happy the message had got through was in face-face talks with the team members. While my style changes to suit the environment of each assignment, my philosophy remains the same – 'explain why you are there . . . then listen'."*

Another said:

*"You have to spend a lot of time with people in a turnaround talking, pushing, reassuring . . . you have to change agendas."*

The best turnaround leaders attempt to share understanding and decision making early in the turnaround process. They recognise that turnaround work is a people thing . . . that it's about getting staff inside the company to trust and believe in them.

# Building the New Team

The new leader must be careful not to be influenced by personal feelings towards individuals. It is not unusual for individuals who are deeply committed (and of value to) the organisation to be ve-hemently opposed to the change of leader or direction, perhaps out of misguided loyalty to the previous CEO or a failure to grasp the nature of the crisis. If the new leader can persuade them to give their support, they may in time become powerful advocates of change.

However, time is very limited and more typically the leader has to reach a decision quickly and let them go. As Calvyn Gardner, the turnaround leader at South Africa's Trans Hex Group, noted:

> *"The most important thing is to take decisive action under less than ideal circumstances. One simply cannot wait for better information, better economic conditions, better personnel or psychometric profiling of your senior management team – nothing is ever perfect and waiting for perfect conditions invariably leads to missing out on what might be good enough to survive and begin to improve."*

Gardner also acknowledges that it can be worth while winning over key individuals if they are of long-term value to the business. Box 4.2 describes the situation that Gardner found at Trans Hex and the style of leadership he provided.

---

**Box 4.2    New Leadership at Trans Hex Group**

Trans Hex Group (THG) is the second largest diamond mining company in South Africa but only a fraction of the size of DeBeers. In September 2001 Calvyn Gardner, who had a track record of turning around companies within the Anglo American Group, was brought in as CEO. He found a company with little or no cash reserves, extensive debt and mines that were nearly at the end of their productive life cycles with no new mining prospects on the immediate horizon. Employee morale was poor with high staff turnover and long-time company veterans quitting. Relationships with the mining unions were extremely poor (see Box 6.2). Adding to these problems was a complete hiatus in the all-important US diamond market following the September 11 attacks.

However, Gardner's diagnostic review determined that THG had the right conditions for growth, in part due to the political change in South Africa. *"What was needed was a structure to support the growth. . . . What I was asked to do was put a plan in place to achieve the turnaround."*

Gardner's immediate focus was on crisis stabilisation. He was relentless in implementing centralised cash management

controls and initiating draconian cost controls. This caused
some disgruntlement among the managers and Gardner moved
swiftly to remove those "deemed unsuitable to the new environment". Others elected to leave of their own accord, but even
then he did not bring in many new people. One situation provided a particular insight into Gardner's style.

One who resigned was Altie Krieger. Altie Krieger, a mining
specialist and 25-year veteran of Trans Hex, was sympathetic
to the mine managers he oversaw, many of whom were up in
arms at seeing organisational power transferred away from the
mines – where it clearly belonged, in their view – and given over
to remote finance managers at company headquarters. Krieger
protested Gardner's changes in a somewhat heated conversation
that led to his resignation.

But Gardner felt Krieger to be a highly desirable asset, and
while Trans Hex would survive without him if it must, Gardner
wanted Krieger on board. As Gardener recounts that episode,
he called Krieger into his office, subsequent to Krieger's resignation – after tempers had cooled – and explained to him
that without the changes that were being instituted, the company faced failure, and those Krieger sought to protect would
be without jobs altogether. Krieger had a choice: leave, or stay
and help those he cared for to turn the company around and improve their own personal circumstances in the process. Krieger
decided to stay and became Director of Land Operations for
the company.

Two years later, Krieger said of Gardner simply, but with a
distinct note of admiration, "he's tough". He seemed further
impressed with Gardner as he described how Gardner spent
time on the ground, visiting every mine, and getting familiar
with every detail, no matter how small or how technical. Trained
as an engineer, Gardner also won praise from Krieger for his
ability to grasp the technical issues involved in running a mine.
"He's tough, but he's fair, and he really understands every aspect of
what's going on here," said Krieger.

When asked about this, Gardner said:

"If you want to be a team player, then you've got to know
what's going on, no matter where it is. You've got to be tuned

*in to what's going on. And that just means putting the effort in. Again, like the captain of the team, you must train probably harder than all the others. And in our case, getting responsibility down (throughout the various levels of the organisation) was absolutely critical. It was impossible to control from the centre. All I could do was try to at least understand what was going on, and then when advice was needed, I could give it. You've got to get your people on board as a team, so that together you can 'stop the bleeding'."*

And getting a handle on costs is where that process must inevitably begin. Gardner told us:

*"Cost control is one of the easy fixes. You've got to cut costs and capex to boost your margins. We implemented cost controls at all levels. We got all the contractors and suppliers in and gave them an ultimatum: we said, 'If you want to supply to us, I want to see a 10% drop in your cost to supply to this company. Otherwise, you're off the list. If I die, you're going to die with me, and what's the point?' We put a huge amount of effort into doing that."*

And this process must be closely monitored so as to determine the level of success – the size of the window of opportunity – it is creating for you.

*"At the end of the day, it's all about measurement: if you start measuring your costs, you find you can manage them."*

Once he'd stemmed the cash outflow at Trans Hex and had control over the liability side of his balance sheet, Gardner focused on what he clearly felt to be his most critical asset: his core team of people.

*"Initially, that was a small group, but we slowly grew an executive team that joined the crusade. We took the view that you were either part of the solution or part of the problem. If you were part of the problem you faced something of an 'exit strategy'. In those beginning days my style was probably dictatorial."*

Gardner was unequivocal in asserting that being dictatorial was not only appropriate, but necessary.

*"If there were any mistakes in those days it was that we didn't make more drastic personal changes. We probably gave a few*

*individuals a little bit too much rope. I always like to believe that you can give someone a chance, but I'm afraid I would recommend that if you do go in [to manage a turnaround] you must be absolutely sure that the team you are working with fully believes that this process can work. You only have a few people who can sound the rallying cry – you can't have guys that you think are on board and really are not. It's just too disruptive."*

After initial tensions, Altie Krieger became one of those changed agents who'd sound the rallying cry. Today he echoes Gardner's concern for getting the people right. Throughout our interview, Gardner stressed the importance of this point: more than simply taking control, he had to create conditions under which his people could – and would want to – understand and implement the changes that were necessary to turn the company around. Communications and leading by example were crucial to that task, and Gardner's approach to this aspect of his turnaround challenge reflected his strong predisposition towards the primacy of the "stakeholder" philosophy over the financial focus that perhaps typifies many US and UK turnaround executives.

*See Boxes 6.2 and 9.3 for further discussion of the Trans Hex turnaround.*

In addition to identifying and removing obvious insurgents or incompetents, the other key considerations in evaluating who to remove and who to keep are the relevance of their management skills to the future of the organisation and their current value – for example, relationships with key customers or critical technical knowledge. If the turnaround leader has had the opportunity to observe management for several weeks in the course of a diagnostic review, he or she may already have identified the "stayers" and "goers" and planned to fill any resulting gaps with interim resource where necessary. Without prior knowledge, he or she may choose to defer changes of senior personnel for several weeks and ensure that adequate resources are in place to mitigate the risks of change. Loss of corporate knowledge is an issue that leaders take into account but rarely is

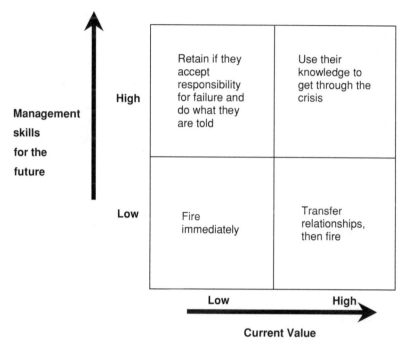

**Figure 4.1**   Reviewing the management.

this a significant issue. Figure 4.1 provides a simple decision-making framework.

The key question on which to judge a management team is: Are they competent to address the task they now face rather than spend too much time judging what they have done in the past.

> " Although I had received detailed evaluations on all staff from former management and investigating accountants, many of their evaluations recommended the replacement of what turned out to be some of the most valuable people to the turnaround process. . . . You have to keep an open mind."

In the majority of situations, the leader has to rely a great deal on his or her intuition and experience in putting together an appropriate team:

> "You must be able to understand people's strengths and weaknesses almost intuitively. Being able to understand and do this on the job is

*crucial. People in a company are essentially all part of a team, albeit a dysfunctional team, but it's your job to bring this team together so they can perform."*

*"If you're creating a team you need to hire people that are complementary to you. I won't go without people who add to my skills – like a capable accountant because I am not an accountant. It's a fool that goes in with the macho style and just blindly says 'do this, do that my way'."*

*"I look people in the eye and decide if I can work with them."*

*"When you bring in new people make sure that the people who are there do not feel that you are parachuting a new team in because they are at fault. . . . What you are doing is complementing existing skills with new skills."*

Practitioners unanimously recommend swift action to deal with resistors and objectors, as there is no time to be wasted in dealing with in-fighting or politicking. It is important to be seen to take action and confirm the authority vested in the new leader:

*"Sometimes you have to be seen to be taking out people who are part of the problem. You generally find three types of people; real dogs, real stars and a big population of in-betweens that are highly sceptical and need to be convinced of the plan. People make up their minds about you (as the turnaround leader) in the first 30–60 days. People have to see change and you have to be seen to be dealing with problem individuals."*

*"If you get a nasty feeling someone is not on your side, get rid of them."*

*"Don't fight with anybody; you have to carry them with you or move them out . . . you lose momentum if you stop and fight."*

*"It's a waste of time trying to manage those that don't want to help . . . it is far easier to fire them."*

*"I give people some limits and constraints. Some don't like this because they're used to operating with a lot of free reign. If people don't like it and can't change they go."*

If someone is behaving inappropriately, you let them go as quickly as possible but you have to be careful:

> *"Firing someone too soon could send the wrong signal . . . that you are not listening or haven't bothered to assess the situation before taking action. It's important to find the right balance . . . somewhere between two weeks and a couple of months is usually about right."*

> *"You have to be sensitive to people's feelings and insecurity but you do have to be ruthless. You cannot be a nice guy, otherwise everybody is out of a job."*

Putting a credible top team in place that is going to help the leader to achieve the turnaround is the critical first step in any mid-size to large corporate entity. Failed organisations usually require a radical change in senior management. This does not always take place immediately, but even in those rare situations where an organisation in trouble has a lot of talent (as was the case at IBM, for example), significant change still takes place, albeit often at a slightly slower pace. If the turnaround leader is to make more than a few senior management changes, he or she must be aware that a lot of time must be invested in a careful selection process to ensure that quality people are appointed. If the turnaround leader comes in as chairman and the existing chief executive is unsuitable for the turnaround task – as is usually the case – the first priority is to find a new chief executive. This can easily take 6 to 12 months with the chairman playing the role of acting CEO in the interim. The critical leadership task of building a top team is well illustrated by what Archie Norman has done at Energis (see Box 4.3).

---

**Box 4.3    Building a New Top Team at Energis**

Archie Norman, who had led the turnaround at Asda in the early 1990s and before that had been Group finance director during the 1980s' turnaround at Woolworths, was appointed executive chairman of Energis in 2002. Energis had become insolvent with approximately £800 million of debt, but the leading institutions believed that the best way to preserve value was to rescue the UK operations by injecting £150 million of new cash. This was contingent on the appointment of new, credible leadership.

One of Norman's immediate priorities was to establish a new management team capable of taking the enterprise forward. He filled 12 of the 14 top positions with recruits from outside the company. Norman spent a lot of time on the recruitment process ensuring that the backgrounds of likely candidates were thoroughly researched to ensure that both the leadership and management capabilities of the successful candidate(s) would meet the turnaround challenges at Energis. He believes it is appropriate to utilise the support of external experts and adopts a variety of assessment methods, including psychometric tests.

The new chief executive, John Pluthero, had previously been CEO of Freeserve, one of Energis's largest customers. He is described as having "a strong controlling instinct and a strong focus on customers" – exactly the traits required in the Energis turnaround.

Norman recognised that to attract top-quality people to a distressed situation he would have to change the senior management reward system. He put in place an incentive system, which linked personal rewards for the top team to any gain in the enterprise's value beyond £400 million, closely aligning management's interests with the interests of the stakeholders who were supporting the company through its turnaround.

It is not always possible to build a new team, particularly in smaller companies where it is difficult to attract good-quality managers to a distressed situation. Many leaders point out that it is essential to have worked with people before you know what they can do, particularly in a turnaround. In a recovery you must have people you trust – that means working with people with whom you have worked successfully before. As one leader said:

*"You just can't bring them into a turnaround on the basis of references since their background does not fully explain what they can actually do."*

The importance of changing at least a few key people in the management team is acknowledged by virtually all turnaround leaders. Most subscribe to the view *"You can't do anything without people"* and that *"there are no bad troops, only bad generals."*

Changing some of the generals has a remarkable effect on most businesses. Bring in a few good people and the "troops with clear focus and leadership will do the job for you". In looking back on their experiences, turnaround leaders are almost unanimous in saying that they kept some of the old guard too long. Patrick O'Sullivan said:

> *"It took me two years to clear out the senior management team. They all went. . . . It took a year too long. . . . As I had a good sense after six months, I should have taken action earlier."*

## Communicating with the Workforce

It is usual practice to take control from the top but it is vital to communicate at all levels of the organisation as soon as possible, if only to pre-empt or forestall the rumour mill. In public or high-profile companies, the new leader's arrival may have been preceded by weeks of press speculation and industry rumour. In almost all organisations, many employees will be aware that there are difficulties, manifested in unhappy customers, delayed payments to suppliers, inability to get decisions made or approved by senior management or rumours of imminent redundancies. The arrival of the new leader may be interpreted as confirming their worst suspicions or fears, particularly if the departing manager has informed them, as has been known to happen, that his replacement is a bank appointee who is coming to close the company – a receiver or administrator in sheep's clothing!

In single site operations, the new leader will typically address the workforce soon after his arrival. Most prefer to speak to the employees directly and avoid intermediation; they have to ensure that the right message is delivered and also recognise that it is hard for incumbent management to acknowledge their mistakes and the consequent difficulties. In large multinational or multi-site businesses, communications programmes are quickly established, using regional briefings, roadshows, "town hall meetings", conference calls and intranet web sites to communicate regularly and openly with employees.

Whatever the circumstances, successful leaders adhere to the same ground rules:

- Be direct, open and honest.
- Acknowledge their concerns.
- Don't make early promises that you may be unable to keep.

In a crisis, it may be appropriate to use shock tactics, to frighten the workforce into rapid compliance with the new world order. Some turnaround leaders can be extremely blunt, as the following quotes illustrate:

> *"How do you grab people's attention when you first arrive? You say to 500 employees of the company 'you're in deep shit."*

> *"I open my address to the workforce with the words . . . some of you will be going and it will be on the legal minimum I can get away with."*

The risks and benefits of this approach are apparent. It may be possible to shock people into compliance in the short term but it may also make the task of the leader more difficult once the crisis has been stabilised and he or she seeks to empower the workforce to engage in more long-lasting change. If a "tough talking" approach is adopted, it needs to be balanced with a human touch – walking around the factory, talking individually to the foremen, operators, secretaries, etc. As one described it, *"implement brutal changes in a gentle fashion"*.

It is important to identify the key influencers and win them over; and it is important to realise that those with most influence may not be apparent from the organisation chart. For example, in an airline the pilots may be disproportionately influential over both cabin crew and ground staff. In a business with a large minority ethnic workforce, it may be a senior family member, rather than the foreman or union representative, who will hold sway with the other employees. This often means by-passing middle and senior management but, as one practitioner said to us: *"If they can't accept this, they have to leave."*

The best leaders demonstrate their humanity, appealing to their common interest in saving the business. They might use dramatic language or theatrical gestures if necessary to engage with and persuade an audience that will at best be neutral, or at worst cynical and hostile. Rhetoric – choice of words and delivery – can be important, as illustrated by the following comment:

*"Use striking language and harness the feelings of the employees – many of them will know what has to be done, they just want to see that it's ok to act."*

Sometimes it can be helpful to use humour to diffuse the tension:

*"I know what you are all thinking, another fat bastard to pay here. Well you'll be pleased to find out that I'm being paid by the day, not by the pound!"*

This leader's objective is to grab their attention while also putting them somewhat at ease, and he follows this attempt to relax the audience with his key messages. Unintentional humour can have the same effect; showing people that you are human gets them on side. One leader made an impassioned speech to the assembled workforce followed by a dramatic exit – into a coat cupboard, having opened the wrong door. He emerged to find his audience in fits of laughter but quickly turned that to his advantage, following up with questions and discussion to "humanise" the tough speech that had preceded his abortive exit.

Whatever the approach, the desired outcome should be to build confidence in the new leader and convey strongly that things will now be done differently. The leader cannot give the audience all they want – i.e. reassurance that their jobs are safe – but he or she can quash the rumours by addressing them head-on and telling the listeners with blunt honesty what has to be done and that he or she is the right person to do it.

*"Tell them what you are going to do and why it needs to be done... be quite directive and autocratic in the process but in a way that convinces them to have confidence in you."*

*"You don't have to listen to me but I have to be here... if you take my advice we will get through."*

Communications at the beginning of the turnaround are not about rebuilding staff morale. In fact the low point in staff morale may not be reached for 9 or 12 months after the start point, when cost reduction and closures start to bite. A junior manager in one turnaround told us:

> *"The first year was very difficult. There were lots of leaving parties and staff morale was low. However as the second year progressed the atmosphere across the company improved and staff now feel optimistic about its prospects. . . . It has only recently hit home how much staff are being listened to."*

While the direction of the early communication with the workforce from the new leader is largely one way, listening to workforce concerns starts to send an important message, and will most likely differentiate him or her from their predecessor. One company doctor actively solicits negative comments and concerns as he likes to give staff the chance to vent their disappointment at what has happened. He then uses this as an opportunity to outline short-term goals and bring staff into the change process.

In most distressed companies, lay-offs will be necessary and the rhetoric one chooses to communicate in these circumstances is critical. Some turnaround leaders prefer to emphasise how they are preserving jobs than talk to the employees about "cutting jobs".

# Setting New Ground Rules

The role of the leader in the crisis stabilisation phase is covered in more detail in Chapter 5. However, it is notable that the majority of turnaround leaders establish the new ground rules within hours rather than days or weeks, reflecting the crisis environment in which they typically operate. New rules of engagement are quickly established from the outset – from the behaviour expected of the management team through to cash controls, information needs and reporting requirements – and it is made clear that these rules are non-negotiable.

The new leader's arrival will evoke a wide range of emotions – fear, anger, cynicism, and resentment – but normally there is also relief that the situation is now 'in hand' and optimism, however guarded, that he or she will lead the company out of its crisis. The audience need not like the message or indeed the messenger but they will be reassured by the calm and confidence born of experience.

## Summary

The leader's first task is to take (and be seen to take) control as quickly as possible. While taking the helm, he or she must also galvanise the crew into taking action to start turning the ship around. The leader must first command; persuasion and discussion come later. To use a military analogy, in peacetime, the army can rely on management techniques – administration, processes and controls – but at times of war, the leader cannot "manage" his troops into battle, he must lead them. This is achieved by:

- Establishing de facto control – normally by removing the incumbent CEO.

- Quickly evaluating senior management and building a top team.

- Communicating directly with all levels of the organisation.

- Remaining calm, confident, utterly determined and dispassionate.

# 5

# Crisis Stabilisation

**H**AVING ESTABLISHED MANAGEMENT CONTROL ON ARRIVAL, the new leader must quickly assert control over the business and take whatever emergency actions are necessary to stabilise the situation. The leader's key task is to ensure the short-term survival of the business while retaining sufficient critical mass to have a viable platform for long-term recovery. At the crisis stabilisation stage, the combination of management and leadership that is particularly required of turnaround leaders is most apparent.

> *"Things don't just happen because you say they've got to happen, but because you ensure they happen."*

On arrival the turnaround leader has a number of immediate management tasks to accomplish:

- to determine or confirm the current financial position (which may have already been assessed in the diagnostic review);

- to establish financial control (through new processes and procedures if necessary); and

- to take whatever actions are necessary to generate cash.

Turnaround leaders have to be wholly detail oriented and hands-on at this stage and cannot delegate responsibility for their most important task – cash management.

Due to the urgency of the problem several initiatives are likely to be launched concurrently at the start of a turnaround. The turnaround leader needs to carefully select trusted individuals to lead the various task forces, such as working capital management and other short-term cash-generating or cost-saving initiatives. He or she should lead these various initiatives while remaining very close to the detail of each activity. The leader may need to convene several progress meetings each day with the team leaders during the early stages of the exercise.

Leadership during crisis stabilisation requires the leader and the team to focus on cash control and operational efficiency. In undertaking these tasks the turnaround leader may be wise to take good legal advice regarding some of the priorities and deals that have to be made. As a director (or even shadow director) the leader has both an ethical and a legal obligation not to continue trading and, in particular, not to incur further credit if the company cannot meet its obligations.

We have identified five key leadership tasks in the crisis stabilisation phase:

- Grabbing the control levers

- Taking tough decisions

- Maintaining visible leadership

- Delivering quick wins

- Dealing with dissent.

### Grabbing the Control Levers

As every turnaround leader knows, businesses don't fail when they run out of profit. They fail when they run out of cash. Therefore, the absolute priority is to stem the outflow of cash, both by identifying additional sources of cash and by drastically reducing payments. The other key levers to be controlled are costs and commitments, as these will convert to cash flows in the near future.

The leader's approach to controlling the levers will vary depending on the size and nature of the business, the severity of the crisis and his or her personal style. There are usually four key steps:

- Establishing controls

- Setting targets

- Measuring results.

- Continuous vigilance

*Establishing Controls*

In a smaller or single-site business, establishing controls may be as simple as seizing cheque books and credit cards and informing all managers that no payments or expenditure can be incurred without the new leader's approval. In multi-site or international companies, this is not usually practical. More commonly, controls are established through drastically reducing delegated authority limits, freezing capital expenditure, recruitment, and even marketing or tendering activity until the business has been stabilised.

Establishing tight controls over cash is the absolute priority. As an experienced practitioner reports, his approach to financial control is:

> *"Draconian ... we grip, grip, grip. We search for exact clarity on the financials. This is where we can wake up dead before we realise what's actually happened to us. We focus on cash, cash and cash."*

Another says:

> *"I will scour the business for things to sell, and personally decide which suppliers need paying and those that can wait. I control all ordering and focus very carefully on stocks and debtors ... I look at every aspect of the cash cycle and work it to the favour of the company. Cash is the lifeblood of any turnaround. In the early days I have a daily meeting, focused only on cash."*

The leader is dependent on the creativity and resourcefulness of his employees to find a multitude of ways to generate and conserve cash. Many impose cash rationing, forcing the business to struggle from day to day with the bare minimum of funding in order to motivate managers to come up with creative ways to survive. Once controls have been established, it has to be made clear that there are no exceptions and that the sanctions for non-compliance are severe, usually involving the immediate firing of the offender.

Experienced practitioners know what they are going to do before arriving. As one said:

> *"I have a set of tools, routines, methods that are not negotiable ... they have to be implemented because they are critical in getting control of the business."*

*Setting Targets*

Leaders employ a variety of approaches to setting targets for the company; their approach being influenced by the severity of the crisis as much as by personal style or preference.

*"In a company in distress, employees need first targets, then a vision."*

Some prefer to set hard targets that must be achieved, for example fixed percentage reductions in costs or absolute headcount reductions. The leader may feel it necessary to supervise closely both how the targets are set and the necessary implementation, as there is little scope to get it wrong. Targets must stretch the organisation, using what one leader calls *"audacious goals"*. If the targets fall short of what is necessary to save the business, failure will be a self-fulfilling prophecy. In our experience we have rarely, if ever, seen a company take cost reduction actions that were too drastic. This requires the leader to push and challenge managers well beyond their comfort zone, and is echoed by one of the practitioners we interviewed:

> *"You can't cut twice. Its got to hurt, senior management have got to lie awake at night wondering if the company can operate now that so much has been cut out. Take out 20% more than they say they can live with."*

At the other end of the spectrum, there are leaders who prefer to guide rather than dictate, to set rules or criteria rather than specific targets, and to rely on the knowledge and capability of management and employees to develop appropriate initiatives and targets. For this approach to be effective, the criteria must be simple and objective. A good example is provided by David Hoare, a highly experienced turnaround practitioner, who sets the following rules:

- If the action simplifies the business and generates cash you don't need tell me – do it.

- If it complicates the business and uses cash, don't even come to me.

- If it complicates the business and generates cash, let's talk.

- If it simplifies the business and uses cash, let's talk.

Simplifying the business is common to the majority of turnarounds. One leader described this as the essence of his role:

> *"I like to get things simple – to kill complexity – to reduce the issues to 3 or 4 key problems and then solve them."*

Another said:

> *"There is a huge amount of focus on knocking a few things over . . . I can fix problems if I hit them hard enough."*

Even at British Telecom, Sir Christopher Bland, the new chairman appointed in 2001, said he made a list of 10 things to do soon after arrival:

> *"Don't have more than 10 things in your list and make sure they are the things that really count."*

## Measuring Results

Finally, the leader must establish robust but simple measurement procedures to ensure that initiatives are yielding results and that targets are met:

> *"At the end of the day it's all about measurement; if you start measuring your costs you find you can manage them."*

Distressed companies often have dysfunctional or ineffective information systems, particularly where multiple IT platforms are in operation, perhaps as a consequence of earlier business acquisitions. The leader cannot allow the absence of good systems to deter the immediate implementation of effective (not necessarily 100% accurate) financial controls. A simple "workaround" system, often based on spreadsheets rather than complex software, can be a critical tool if the leader is to receive timely and accurate information. All competent turnaround leaders establish a few key metrics and then monitor these frequently – usually weekly and often daily in a cash crunch.

## Continuous Vigilance

Having established controls, targets and measurement systems, the leader must then adapt continuously to events and issues as they arise. While controls must be rigorously enforced, targets are rarely static but are updated or amended to reflect changing circumstances. For example, if sales decline or a major customer is lost, further cost reductions may be required to achieve at least a break-even position. If a major supplier demands payment in advance, compensating cash savings will have to be found to meet the additional funding needs. Experienced turnaround practitioners expect constant change as a matter of course, building contingency plans and evolving their decisions in response to the ever-changing circumstances. Equally important, turnaround leaders must not become wedded to a single idea or solution; if something is not working, they must adapt or abandon it and find other solutions. Turnaround leaders are not, by their nature, over-confident or over-optimistic but tend to be downside managers, anticipating the worst while motivating people to give their best.

*"Constant review and reassessment of options, you will never do exactly what you started out to do, you can't think in absolutes. Don't let it go to inertia. You need to have a lot of things moving at once, some will work, others will fail. We're not magicians."*

At Marconi, Mike Parton held weekly reviews of all key performance indicators for many months after he became CEO (see Box 5.1).

---

**Box 5.1    Control and Crisis Stabilisation at Marconi**
*(See Box 4.1 for background to the Marconi turnaround)*

Mike Parton introduced draconian controls over cash and costs. The absolute priority was to ensure that cash did not run out. Over 100 initiatives were underway to generate or conserve cash. Cash was pooled in "lockboxes", with access requiring both lenders' consent and the CEO's approval. Cash was "rationed" with minimal funding available from the centre, forcing local management to be creative in managing their own cash flows. Actual and projected cash utilisation was monitored weekly.

Mike chaired the weekly cash review himself – an important symbolic and practical demonstration of his leadership in this area.

Cost reduction was masterminded by Mike Donovan, the Chief Operating Officer, who led a world-wide project to reduce the cost base. Every area of expenditure was analysed and targets were set and rigorously monitored to squeeze costs down from an annualised run-rate of £890 million per annum to below £400 million in under two years. Mike Donovan's weekly progress reviews were notorious for their relentless attention to detail, ensuring that every initiative was progressing to plan.

It is at the crisis stabilisation stage that turnaround advisers (as opposed to executives) are most likely to be involved in the operational turnaround. They are available at short notice, and can provide the vital financial management skills that are missing in distressed businesses. They may have been "forced" on the company by the creditors even before a turnaround executive has been appointed, or may be brought in by the turnaround executive if he or she does not have a reliable team to do the work. Advisers need to be firm and effective communicators and remember that they do not have the power of a court-appointed administrator. Their leadership can be fairly low key since most of their communication is with the finance function and the Board, with whom they will be in daily contact. They need to deliver some tangible progress quickly in the cash flow situation to create confidence and stakeholder trust. However, before this can occur advisers have to confront management with the reality of the situation, outline likely crisis points and manage hubris. If advisers are to be effective they usually need to have Board approval to control outgoing expenditure for a fixed period of time, which often involves them over-riding the responsibility of the financial director or controller (see Box 5.2 for a simple example).

### Box 5.2   Stretching Creditors

Upon entering a company, one turnaround adviser realised that a quick win on cash management was "stretching" payments to the creditors. He approached the Board and obtained formal authority to control outgoing operating expenditure for a fixed period of time (reviewable), over-riding the responsibility of the financial controller. This accomplished a number of things:

- It clarified the situation so there was no ambiguity in the creditor environment.

- It allowed a fresh view to be taken of creditor payment priorities and the renegotiation of credit terms.

- It removed the pressure on the existing financial controller as the critical cash flow decisions were taken from him.

- It gave the adviser a credible mandate with which to move forward.

The practitioner was able to control the flow of funds objectively, establish credibility with the Board and give reassurance to all stakeholders about the short-term future.

## Taking Tough Decisions

Common to all crises is a lack of time. In these situations, faced with imperfect information and a multitude of issues clamouring for their attention, how do leaders make decisions? First of all they prioritise the issues they have to tackle and only focus on what is absolutely critical to achieve stabilisation. Turnaround practitioners have to be particularly good at identifying and then focusing on the short-term priorities – to the exclusion of all else – but must remain flexible as they unearth new problems and face unexpected constraints.

All the turnaround leaders we interviewed readily acknowledged that the final responsibility for all decisions must rest with them. Many assume a highly controlling role in the early days of the turnaround, describing their style as "dictatorial" or "highly autocratic":

*"Tell them what you are going to do and why it needs to be done. Be quite directive and autocratic in the process, but in a way that convinces them to have confidence in you."*

*"I had to be strong and single minded... company doctors need to be thick skinned, egocentric, dominant, individuals full of themselves*

*and full of their opinions. This is required when a company is in serious trouble – people have lost the way, management has failed, and the financial situation is precarious. Therefore during this phase you cannot be a team player and support everyone, instead you need to be relatively autocratic and a very strong individual that commands."*

This leadership style is a pragmatic response to the immense pressure in this crisis phase. Others are prepared to delegate some decision making, but remain clearly in control:

*"I want to be in control but I like the team to take decisions when they can. I am not afraid to take decisions and will do so whenever they are required."*

At the other end of the scale, a few leaders expressed the belief that it is not in the long-term interests of the company to allow management to become overly dependent on the leader for decision making. They continuously solicit input and tell employees only to come to them for a final decision. One practitioner makes it clear to his management team that if he is asked to make a decision, then once it is made there is no going back and no appeals are allowed. This forces the organisation as a whole to be more decisive – people are forced to take responsibility if they want to get the outcome they prefer. If such an approach is to be effective, employees must not be afraid to take decisions and although accountable for their actions, the occasional mistake must be tolerated.

Regardless of the approach, successful leaders trust a great deal to experience and intuition in forming their judgements and making decisions. One turnaround leader describes his approach:

*"You use judgement. Most judgement is only evaluated historically. When you're in the storm and you know that you don't have all the factual information that you normally would like to have to apply proper judgement, you still have to make your decision – you are applying decisions that are either right or wrong by only a knife-edge."*

There are usually some glaringly obvious moves when you start the turnaround process, which begs the question why the old management team have not acted. The answer is a switch in focus – caused by the arrival of a new leader who is better able to recognise and respond to the situation as it exists.

Finally, perhaps the most important characteristic of decision making in a crisis is to make the decision, and move on. The leader cannot afford to dwell on each decision. Therefore, however democratic the decision-making process, the outcome must be imposed, autocratically if necessary, on the organisation:

> *"Once the decision is made, there is no room for further discussion. You can't leave any room for changes or a different direction."*

However, turnaround leaders stress the need to be flexible since not everything you try will work:

> *"You need constant review and reassurance of options... you will never do what you started out to do. You're constantly re-looking at the decision tree. You need to have a lot of things moving at once... some will work others will fail. We're not magicians."*

Turnaround leaders are pragmatic. They recognise when a course of action is not working, stop it and reprioritise other ideas or projects.

### Maintaining Visible Leadership

As the turnaround progresses, it may become appropriate for the leader to retire somewhat into the background, allowing the management team to become the visible face of the leadership. At this stage, however, the leader must be visibly in command, leading from the front, chairing difficult meetings and addressing problems real-time, preferably face-to-face. The leader will build on the communication processes described in Chapter 4, exemplifying the actions and conduct he or she expects from the team.

Typically, the company will be in a fast-changing, near-chaotic environment. The employees, most of whom will never have experienced a crisis before, may be shocked, resentful and fearful and will need firm guidance and reassurance to ensure them that they are doing the right things. One turnaround leader said:

*"You have to spend a lot more time with people in turnaround situations – talking, pushing, reassuring . . . you have to align agendas."*

Another advises:

*"Smother them with your presence, be there all the time."*

This proximity to the employees is vital, not only to ensure that the turnaround leader remains focused on the key tasks necessary for survival, but also to ensure the employees that he or she is aware of problems and issues and is positioned to take swift corrective action. One turnaround practitioner recalled turning up on the night shift where he checked the time cards and looked for every single worker. He soon found people sleeping or clocked in but nowhere to be found. A few redundancies later the message sank in and workers started "taking care of the shirkers themselves".

All successful turnaround leaders lead by example, demonstrating what they require of their employees through their own behaviour, both in words and actions. After the initial communication process, the next key interaction with the majority of the employees is usually the redundancy process, as costs are cut to save the business. The way in which this is managed and the leavers are treated will have a significant influence on the morale and loyalty of remaining employees and their perception of the new leader.

*You need to implement brutal changes in a gentle fashion. Make it as easy as possible for those who leave . . . err on the side of generosity and fairness."*

Keeping track of what happens to those who leave (to the extent possible) and "communicating about this internally to show that they were not coldly abandoned", was an approach mentioned by several practitioners.

Leading by example provides a strong catalyst for changing the norms and ways of doing things within the firm. Being on time at meetings, delivering tasks on time, treating all employees with respect and saying "I don't know" are all examples of actions which when taken together, start to change the organisational culture. Consistency along with integrity are critical leadership attributes if trust is to be built quickly.

Throughout the crisis stabilisation the turnaround leader maintains clear and open communication both internally and externally. Some develop a clear communication programme, sometimes with the help of external advisers, to describe "where we are and what we'll do by when". Providing a time frame serves this purpose. It helps to reduce feelings of uncertainty and bolsters the leader's credibility if actions are completed on or ahead of schedule. Clear communications complete with real results are what both employees and external stakeholders want. In communicating action plans for crisis stabilisation, turnaround leaders often communicate the consequences of failure so that people (both internally and externally) understand the reasons behind decisions and actions. As one said:

> *"You have to make them see that you will be cutting off a leg, the only question is, which one?"*

## Delivering Quick Wins

Most turnaround leaders seek early wins. It is good for employees' morale, and gives a sense of achievement and renewed momentum. Companies in distress typically enter a downward spiral of over-promising and under-delivering. It is the leader's task to reverse this trend and restore confidence in the business by ensuring that the company delivers against its promises, be they to customers, suppliers, employees or lenders.

Opportunities for early wins may be readily apparent to the employees but someone needs to ask them – and then listen. As we have said earlier, many turnaround leaders recognise that "the workers know what is wrong with the company and they know how to fix it. The problem is that no one ever bothers to ask them."

While quick wins are nice to have and start to generate momentum, they are by themselves usually insufficient to stabilise the company, and more drastic action is required. Nevertheless, turnaround leaders recognise the need for quick wins and help their people to achieve this:

> *"I look for quick wins. I encourage people to bring me their problems and help them to analyse them and sort them out. I then try to coach them to come up with their own solutions next time . . . when I probe them: Is this your responsibility? What do you suggest?"*

> *"If you want quick wins look no further than the HR department and internal communications . . ."*

Employees must be encouraged to achieve quick wins – they will not do it without support from the top. In recent years there has been a tendency for companies to set challenging top-down targets (BHAGs – big hairy audacious goals) to stretch the organisation to think more innovatively. This can be wrong in a turnaround situation where employee confidence is likely to be low. Where managers and staff are encouraged to set their own goals, turnaround practitioners sometimes find staff being over-ambitious. They try to impress their new bosses by setting tough goals, but then fail to achieve them, which is not helpful to anyone. The secret is actually to breakdown challenging goals into a series of smaller steps – and as the first steps are achieved, momentum develops and the steps can get bigger. This is essentially what happens in the GE Work Out Process used by Patrick O'Sullivan in the turnaround of Eagle Star and Zurich (see Box 9.2 for more details).

One turnaround leader came into a business in distress, where the company had fallen behind in delivering a consignment of half a million potted Christmas trees to Asda. As with all seasonal products, there was a limited window of opportunity and the consequences of any failure to deliver were potentially disastrous, affecting both short-term cash and the longer term relationship with a major customer. The new leader spent time talking to the workers and was eventually told that the major bottleneck was the root trimming process, as the company had only three pairs of shears between 30 men. He went straight to a nearby garden centre, purchased 30 new pairs of shears (so that three were not left with the old ones!), distributed them to the workers and enabled them to catch up on the delivery schedule. This simple act ensured that the order was fulfilled and also helped to restore the morale of the workforce.

Another practitioner was appointed to turnaround a playground equipment manufacturer. The company had installed equipment on behalf of a developer in a construction project for a local government entity. The developer had refused to pay the manufacturer until he had been paid by his customer, the local authority. This had dragged on for some time and the equipment manufacturer was now experiencing a liquidity crisis. The new leader was aware that the developer could not get paid by his customer unless the equipment was correctly installed and approved by the customer. He therefore instructed his employees to return to the site and cut away and remove all the playground equipment, leaving 4-inch metal stubs in place of the swings and slides! The developer quickly paid up, relieving the cash crisis at the equipment manufacturer and the playground was duly re-installed.

## Dealing with Dissent

Turnaround leaders are unanimous in how to deal with overt dissent: swiftly and ruthlessly. If the boat is to stay afloat and move forward, there is no room for those who want to paddle in a different direction. The approach to changing senior management, described in Chapter 4, applies everywhere in the organisation as the turnaround progresses. There are other ways in which dissent or non-compliance can disrupt the crisis stabilisation process. Box 5.3 – the Tea Huts Story – provides an interesting anecdote of how one turnaround leader dealt with resistance to change.

---

### Box 5.3   Tea Huts Story

Jim Carter, a turnaround practitioner, had been approached by a major lending bank to help a distressed company in the commercial ship maintenance industry. It was losing about £2 million p.a. on a turnover of £8 million and was facing a serious liquidity crunch. Having been appointed as Managing Director, Jim quickly identified that the key to survival of the business was improved productivity through multi-tasking and flexible working. Having communicated the dire financial situation to the 250 strong workforce – each of whom was a union member in one of five different trade unions – Jim eventually

---

persuaded them that there was no alternative to these changes if the company was to avoid liquidation. The next step was to deal with certain cherished but deeply unproductive working practices.

The site was spread across 40 acres of land dotted with "tea huts" – portacabins where the men stored various tools, complete with hot drink vending machines and pornographic decorations. Whenever a worker needed a particular tool, he would embark upon an expedition, searching the various tea huts and enjoying a few hot drinks on the way. Jim decided that this had to end. He set up two easily accessible, large canteens complete with vending machines and microwaves and set a deadline. The workers had three weeks to remove their belongings and dismantle the tea huts. Three weeks passed and the workers continued to wander between the tea huts as before.

Jim therefore ordered a mobile crane that was working on the site to pick up the nearest tea hut, carry it to the dump-yard and dump it. The crane crew initially refused; Jim insisted, telling them: "*Do it or I'll climb up into the crane and do it myself.*" The hut was duly dumped. The news spread through the site like wildfire; within 5 minutes every worker knew what had happened and the remaining tea huts were quickly emptied and dismantled.

It can be far more difficult to detect and take action against passive or covert dissent. It can take several weeks or months to discover that individuals are paying enthusiastic lip-service to the new regime while obstructing or undermining initiatives through passive non-co-operation or mis-communication to their subordinates. Patrick O'Sullivan at Zurich Financial Services refers to these dissenters as the "permafrost", getting between the business and the new leader. Jack Welch described them as those who "kiss up and kick down". Experienced leaders seek to prevent this from happening by disintermediation – frequent communication of the facts, direct to the workforce, without allowing "interpretation" or corruption of their message. Good communications can be hard to sustain through a crisis, when there are many other imperatives, but it is the surest way of cutting through the "permafrost". In addition, offenders have to be removed without hesitation, both to set an example to the organisation and to remove any credibility from their previous actions or words.

# Summary

- "Benign dictatorship" is the most common leadership style during crisis stabilisation, but motivating employees and having access to their knowledge, creativity and initiative requires a fine balance between authority and autocracy.

- Asserting control is the essential leadership task in a crisis. This is usually the most "management-like" of the leadership tasks, requiring the establishment of controls and targets and continuous measurement of results.

- Leaders must remain flexible and adaptable, grabbing early wins where they can and changing course as necessary to ensure survival.

- Dissent cannot be tolerated and should be swiftly and ruthlessly eliminated.

- Leaders must practise visible leadership through their presence and communications. Successful leaders acknowledge that they "can change everything and sustain nothing" without the support and buy-in of the people around them.

# 6

# Stakeholder Management

TROUBLED COMPANIES NEED TWO THINGS; STRONG LEADER-
ship and capital. Stakeholders include the owners and providers
of capital to the business and stakeholder management is at the core
of a turnaround: it is the engine oil that allows the turnaround process
to occur. It is a critical leadership task in any organisation and never
more important than in a crisis.

In Chapter 3 we discussed gaining support among key financial stakeholders for a turnaround and the leadership role that can be played
by lenders and other financial stakeholders. This chapter addresses
the critical role of maintaining stakeholder support throughout the
turnaround process, and the key role that the turnaround executive
plays in this process.

The nature of this task will depend on the number of classes of stakeholder as well as the relationship between the stakeholders. While
it is the financial stakeholders that tend to have the decision-making
power in a financial restructuring, other stakeholder groups, in particular customers and employees, ultimately determine whether a turnaround is successful and there are others whose support is necessary
to allow the turnaround process to work. These include the Board of
directors, key suppliers, trade unions, government and even the press
– in fact "anyone who can have a negative effect on your cash flow".

## Bridging the Gap

When a crisis erupts in the corporate world very few of the top executives have "been there before". In contrast, many of their financial
stakeholders have previous experience of turnaround situations and
often have strong opinions on what needs to happen. As a result,

there is frequently an enormous mismatch of experience and expectation and a blame culture soon develops. In these circumstances, the role of the turnaround practitioner is to bridge the expectations gap between the disgruntled financial stakeholders ("management is incompetent") and disillusioned management ("what is wrong with these bankers, they were fine when things were going well and now it rains a little and they want all their umbrellas back").

It requires considerable leadership skill to realign these two groups. Patience and listening skills are a prerequisite to establishing a mutual understanding of the nature of the problem. Turnaround and restructuring is much more likely to be successful if there is mutual agreement among all the affected stakeholders as to the true financial and operational position of the business.

At this stage the turnaround practitioner, whether turnaround executive or adviser, needs to undertake a critical task – his or her analysis of stakeholder positioning (see Box 6.1)

---

### Box 6.1   Analysing Financial Stakeholders

- Who they are.

- What rights they believe they have.

- What rights they actually have.

- What interconnectivities there are, if any, between stakeholders.

- What they consider the key issues to be.

- What they consider the options to be both for themselves and for the company.

- What realistic options they have.

- What alternative options the company has and the extent to which the company is a key player or influencer in pursuing one or other option.

- A worst case, or liquidation analysis that shows what each stakeholder could achieve or expect in the event of a liquidation of the business.

Stakeholder positioning analysis is an iterative process, reflecting new knowledge about the company's position as it becomes available and the changing "temperature" of the stakeholder "pool". Typically the turnaround practitioner will check his or her analysis with the stakeholders and test his or her understanding of their position. The objective is to reach an understanding of "Where are we now?" because it is only from a common understanding and agreement of the base position that a consensus can be established and turnaround can begin. Successful turnaround practitioners know as much or more about stakeholders' options than the stakeholders or their representatives. Once it is demonstrated that the stakeholders are the most knowledgeable players, they are then often trusted with developing a participation process, which balances the rights and requirements of all those involved and is mutually respected.

Typically, the stakeholder positioning analysis will be conducted in parallel with the completion of the diagnostic review and communication of the review findings to the key stakeholders.

The role of the turnaround practitioner is to understand the needs of the company and the requirements of the stakeholders and to find an alignment that both can live with. This is not always easy. Finding an acceptable solution among the key financial stakeholders requires the rebuilding of consensus from within an environment of blame and distrust. This can be a long drawn out process which requires considerable "consensual" leadership skills. The practitioner may have to invest time to help individual stakeholders to deal with difficult issues or concerns, but must ensure that he or she never becomes, or is perceived to be, a puppet or spokesperson of any of the stakeholders or pushes a position too hard. The more autocratic turnaround executives may find this need for a consensual style difficult and become frustrated by the time consumed in the process. Nonetheless, failure to build consensus will jeopardise the turnaround.

The perception of bias in favour of a particular stakeholder group can become a significant obstacle to the restructuring process. The turnaround practitioner usually represents the company and has a duty to all stakeholders, particularly if he or she is employed as the chairman or chief executive, or in another official role. The role of advisers can be less clear-cut. Typically in US and UK restructuring situations (although not in continental Europe), the majority of the advisers are introduced by the creditors but are paid for by the company. Such advisers are often perceived as being closely aligned with the interests of particular stakeholders – even if they are ostensibly working for the corporate – because the financial stakeholders represent a source of repeat business for them. This can strain relationships with management and erode the quality of information received from them to facilitate the process.

In complex financial restructurings, it is increasingly common for each major financial stakeholder group to have its own legal and financial advisers and for a Chief Restructuring Officer to be appointed to act impartially and objectively for the corporate and all its stakeholders, and to play an honest broker role at the centre. The experienced practitioner respects the rights and views of the financial stakeholders, in particular the creditors who often have the major economic interest in the entity, but does not compromise his or her reputation or credibility by exhibiting bias or preference for any stakeholder group.

# Financial Stakeholders

The characteristic common to all of financial stakeholders in a turnaround, be they providers of debt or equity, is that their economic interest is at risk to a greater extent than anticipated when they invested in the enterprise.

A successful turnaround for any stakeholder who finds himself in this position is one that returns the risk profile of the company, as seen from the perspective of the stakeholder, to that which they find acceptable to enable them to continue to participate in the business of the company. It is often presumed, usually erroneously, that all financial stakeholders simply want their money back. More often they are willing to remain involved and invested, but on the terms for which they gave approval when they initially became committed.

In Chapter 3 we discussed the critical diagnostic phase. That is important since you cannot begin to solve a problem until you understand it and have identified its root causes. Complete knowledge is a luxury rarely available to a turnaround practitioner. The practitioner has to act on the basis of the knowledge available. The more experienced will operate in such a way as to make progress without being committed to a course of action that may be attractive to one stakeholder but will subsequently be offensive to another. He or she will endeavour to plot the course that maintains viability of the enterprise while causing the least offence to all stakeholders in light of their statutory or contractual rights. This is inevitably a difficult course to steer. The process is essentially one of obtaining a balance and it is unlikely that the final balance that is achieved would have been acceptable had it been presented to all stakeholders at the outset. This is because not only is the turnaround practitioner developing an approach based on a knowledge of the facts, but so too are all the affected stakeholders. The affected stakeholders need to obtain a knowledge of the position, prospects and plan that enable them to support the general shape of a proposed restructuring. Many hours are spent on stakeholders negotiating marginal benefits at the cost of others but, to a certain extent, it is all a side show . . . frustrating as that may be.

If a breakthrough is to be achieved it will depend on the leadership exhibited by the turnaround practitioner in understanding the positions and options of all the affected stakeholders, obtaining their trust, and introducing enough transparency into the process to enable each to generally understand the position of the others. To those outside the process, many restructurings appear to take a long time yet to those engaged in the process the pressure of time is often felt to be overbearing.

This circumstance arises because each stakeholder has to move from a prejudice-driven position, where decisions are often based on perception and emotion, to one where decisions are grounded in fact. The turnaround practitioner needs to help to establish the facts as well as guide the stakeholders through the process at different speeds to ensure that, eventually, all are ready to deal at the same time on the same basis. This requires focus, patience and above all the ability of the leader to remain calm, objective and dispassionate throughout.

Integrity and openness are the critical leadership skills in dealing with stakeholders and financial stakeholders in particular. Turnaround leaders typically provide financial stakeholders with full and frank disclosure, finding that "putting all the bad news on the table" helps to build credibility and trust, although it may generate short-term hostility if the financial stakeholders are in denial. It is preferable to go to financial stakeholders with solutions as well as problems, but experienced practitioners know not to delay in sharing information and working with stakeholders to reach an informed consensus.

## Inter-stakeholder Relationships

The management of inter-stakeholder relationships between different financial institutions, both within a creditor class (for example, senior secured lenders) and between different classes of creditors, can become exceedingly complex. In the past, when a company got into difficulty it typically had long-standing relationships with one or two lenders who would either support it towards a solution or push it into insolvency. Now even mid-sized corporates may have complex capital structures with several types of syndicated and bilateral loans, high-yield debt or mezzanine finance. Furthermore, following the growth of the secondary debt markets, that debt is constantly traded and revalued, resulting in a disparate group of creditors with different motivations. Many will be sub-par investors whose economic interest will not necessarily be the face value of their debt instrument, and their perceptions, degree of knowledge of the company, agendas and objectives will vary considerably.

A key part of stakeholder management is to ensure that the turnaround does not fail because of a failure to reach agreement within or between stakeholder groups. Relationships within a stakeholder class such as a senior lender group are normally governed by the terms of the loan documentation or indenture documentation (for publicly traded debt). Occasionally, relationships between different classes of creditors are governed by an "inter-creditor" agreement which establishes priority over security and prevents one class of creditor from taking precipitative action. It is critical that the creditor groups are led by an experienced co-ordinating committee and more particularly that the co-ordinating committee ("co-com") appoints a chairman who can command the respect and support of the whole group and has the experience to contribute effectively to the development of a solution. Experienced turnaround executives are not afraid to influence the choice of co-com chairman and may even put pressure on creditors to change the chairman if he or she is not providing sufficient leadership of the stakeholders being represented. A good leader works out who the other leaders are.

Experienced turnaround and restructuring practitioners will work with the co-com chairman or syndicate leaders to help to manage conflicts within or between the classes. Just as transparency between the company and its key financial stakeholders is a prerequisite to stakeholder support, so there is a need, in complex cases, for an open relationship between the co-com and the turnaround practitioner. To achieve this the turnaround practitioner needs to develop and maintain the trust of all parties, with regular communication and prompt disclosure of pertinent information. Paul Thompson of HSBC puts it this way:

*"Differing degrees of interest and influence will attach to different stakeholders, between whom there may well be significant tension. To deal with such a sensitive environment the turnaround practitioner needs to disclose the most relevant information. . . . They can avoid unnecessary suspicion and anxiety by seeking support through open discussion."*

Not all turnaround practitioners will have the ability to manage the complexity of stakeholder relationships involved in a multi-banking situation. The nature of the task is summarised by a lead banker as follows:

*"There can be a huge number of banks involved and you can get a relatively small business having 30 banks involved. These banks may not have people in London and the account could be run from New York or Frankfurt. When involved with such a workout, the communication process is something that the lead bank or the leading group of banks need to give considerable thought to. A lot of changes in covenants, changes in terms, etc., often need 100% agreement which means communicating with 20 or 30 banks and persuading them to your viewpoint. However, you may not always have the same agenda as the others if, for example, your exposure via bonds is greater. This exposure issue is never obvious and requires careful handling and relationship building skills."*

This banker emphasises that the resolution of possible disputes and alignment of objectives requires the ability to manage a high-quality communication process across a large group:

> *"This often involves understanding where other people might be coming from, trying to make sure that you give the impression that you are managing the position and keeping a lid on all communications. For instance, I'm not very happy when I read in the* Evening Standard *something that I've not heard through the normal channels."*

Success also requires creating a "no surprise" approach for other stakeholders, particularly banks; a series of shocks and surprises will undermine the credibility of the work-out banker within his or her own institution and make it almost impossible to maintain the support of the individual or the institution he or she represents:

> *"The more shocks and surprises that they get, the more difficult it will be for managers fronting a London based banking relationship to convince the powers that be, in New York or wherever, that this is being managed in the right direction."*

The leadership role that the chairman and members of the co-ordinating committee play is absolutely critical and can make the difference between a failed or successful turnaround. Bankers who are successful in this role are highly experienced and depend heavily on their personal credibility with the other institutions. They will invest time to understand the different agendas of the other lenders in the class and seek a solution that is broadly acceptable. They must be seen to act impartially and not to seek a preferential solution for their own institution, for example, where they have other credits or facilities with the company outside the syndicated debt. With the growth of secondary debt trading, this task is becoming considerably more complex as the participants can change overnight, the risk profile for each constituent can vary sharply and this, of course, determines the attitude they will have to a given situation.

Personal relationships can smoothe the process and it is generally acknowledged within the banking market that "what goes around comes around". In practice, if one bank "holds out" to improve its position, particularly when it has a small exposure and uses it to "hold other banks to ransom", it is unlikely that that bank will make the shortlist for the next lucrative syndication or leveraged transaction or obtain the support of other lenders in a subsequent case, where the bank might have a more substantial exposure.

A successful turnaround requires all stakeholders to reach an aligned position. The turnaround practitioner must work with the chairman and co-ordinating committee of credit classes to ensure that a turnaround is not derailed by inter-creditor conflicts. The turnaround leader may be instrumental in "unblocking" creditor conflicts through direct negotiation with the affected parties.

## Creditors

The support of key suppliers, who are usually unsecured creditors, can be critical to the success of a turnaround. Obtaining and maintaining their support will depend on the credibility of the turnaround team and is underpinned by their reputation for integrity and achieving results. Suppliers have to believe that it is in their interest to continue to supply the business and leave credit lines in place without immediate clarity as to when and how their existing or future debts will be paid. This requires good communication and delivery against any promises made. An experienced practitioner describes it as follows:

*"Relationships with suppliers required individual negotiations. As trade creditors are usually unsecured, requested increases in credit lines from suppliers meant that the suppliers had to feel comfortable that they would be treated fairly and paid. In other words, they had to believe that the new management team was being ethical and straightforward in their dealings. The shared interest in keeping production on schedule meant there was little resistance from suppliers who had large outstanding balances or those that were in highly competitive commodity type ingredients. However, continued deliveries from suppliers of more hard-to-get ingredients required greater flexibility and, at times, legal counsel to make sure that improper preference was not being given to some suppliers over others."*

Dealing with suppliers can be enormously time consuming so the experienced practitioner ranks suppliers according to their importance and manages them accordingly, investing time to develop a relationship at a senior level with key suppliers. If this is not achieved, the turnaround could fail due to lack of supplier support, to the detriment of both the company and the supplier, as the following example illustrates:

> *"I decide which suppliers are needed and then speak to them directly. The creditors that the company doesn't need are ignored. I keep payments to a minimum, cutting deals with important suppliers and ignore those who can be substituted. In dealing with creditors I adopt my normal straightforward blunt style. It is important to find the decision maker in the supplier organisation and adopt a 'say what you mean and mean what you say' attitude. In one case where British Telecom were critical and were owed £80,000 but the company could not afford to pay, I offered 60% in full and final settlement but the structure of BT could not handle this. The offer was rejected and when the company failed BT received nothing."*

### Customers

Customers are, of course, the life blood of any business. Without them there is no business. When word gets out that a key supplier is in difficulties, the key concern for all customers is continuity of supply. In many turnaround situations, the company may have acceptable or even good relations with its customers, in which case continuous reassurance during the crisis phase may be sufficient to maintain the relationship. The following comment from a turnaround executive in a small company is fairly typical:

> *"I always seek to reassure customers of continuation of supply. . . . I usually let the current personnel that interact with customers continue to do so, and will encourage them to keep talking and keep reassuring the customers. . . . However I will get more involved if it is a big customer and big order that will keep the company alive."*

In other situations, particularly in technology-based businesses and some service businesses, the role of the turnaround leader can be critical in securing the support of key customers. Lou Gerstner at IBM, Michael Capellas at MCI, Mike Parton at Marconi and Francisco Caio at Cable & Wireless were all very active in key account management in the early stages of their turnarounds.

At MCI, Michael Capellas realised from the outset that restoring trust with customers (and other stakeholders) was fundamental to the turnaround. As one of his direct reports said to us:

> *"Amazingly enough throughout this whole period, we did not lose a single major customer and managed to maintain industry leading service standards. That's because when Michael Capellas got in, he marshalled the troops and said we have to keep our eye on what's important, and what's important is take care of our customer, doing the right thing for them and for everybody. When given that kind of leadership people make sure that those customers were taken care of. They understood where we were going, what was going on with the bankruptcy, what we were doing in terms of corporate governance and its implementation. They could see with that kind of information that there was a light at the end of the tunnel."*

At IBM Lou Gerstner took a similar approach when he implemented "Operation Bear Hug". After three weeks in the job, he was concerned about the loss of customer trust. To quote from his book:

> *Each of the 50 members of the senior management team was to visit a minimum of five or six biggest customers during the next three months. The executives were to listen, to show the customer that we cared, and to implement holding actions as appropriate. Each of their direct reports, a total of more than 200 executives, were to do the same. For each Bear Hug visit, I asked that a one to two page report be sent to me and anyone else who could solve the customer's problems. . . . Bear Hug became a first step in IBM's culture change . . . the people realised that I really did read every one of the reports, there was great improvement in action and responsiveness.*

While retaining profitable customers is always critical, so is the reverse – "losing" unprofitable customers. Implementing product

---

* Gerstner, L., *Who Says Elephants Can't Dance?*, Harper Collins, 2002.

market refocusing, one of the seven key ingredients of a successful turnaround (see Chapter 7), usually involves cutting out unprofitable product lines as quickly as possible, which may not allow the customer to identify alternative sources within their normal lead time. If the customer is still important to the business – for example, is a buyer of other more profitable products and services – then the turnaround management team has to try to support the customer through the transition.

It can be very difficult for sales people to lead these negotiations as they are not accustomed to saying no to their customers. The turnaround leader may need to circumvent the normal buying process and negotiate directly with senior management in the customer organisation to redefine the parameters and terms of the relationship. Where there has been a history of poor service and the existing customer relationships are damaged, this is also an opportunity to rebuild key relationships by listening and responding to customer concerns.

## Unions and Employees

Confrontation with the unions and employees is relatively rare in turnaround situations in the USA and the UK today, since most union leaders recognise the reality of companies in trouble. Obtaining their support for fundamental change in working practices can still be very difficult and time consuming, but they are nearly always aware of a distressed company's problems and even welcome the arrival of new management.

Changing out-dated working practices in industries with low margins may be critical to the turnaround effort, as was the case at Rolls Royce Motors in the early 1990s. In that situation, and in order to show the union representatives that the status quo was not an option, the management negotiator tore up the existing union agreement in front of them and threatened to close the company unless new flexible multiskilling arrangements were introduced. The judicious use of brinkmanship during negotiations is a common characteristic of turnaround leadership, particularly where a change or decision is regarded as "mission critical".

There is no substitute, however, for a strong communications strategy, good negotiating judgement and lots of patience when dealing with unions. This is particularly true in the public sector where the unions are often the biggest obstacle to change. A Director of Operations and Services in a public sector turnaround recalls meetings *"where a quarter of the time was taken up just keeping the unions informed and two-day activities could take four weeks because the unions wanted to know everything and have everything discussed with them"*.

In less-developed countries, dealing with the unions and the workforce can be significantly more difficult. Ugly confrontations, sometimes spilling over into violence, are not uncommon. In one situation in Argentina, the court-appointed turnaround leader arrived at a bank's headquarters to find the building surrounded by the army and the workforce occupying the executive suite. Through straight talking he persuaded both sides to "go home" and the workforce to return to work the following day.

We talked in Chapter 4 about the need for turnaround leaders to show courage. Fortunately, there are relatively few situations which also require exemplary personal and physical bravery. The turnaround of Trans Hex, the South African diamond mining company (for background see Box 4.2), is one such example.

The workers went out on strike soon after Calvyn Gardner was appointed. The strike turned violent – offices, houses and plants were burned – and at one of the mines workers fired on management (and the fire was returned). Box 6.2 tells the remarkable story of Calvyn Gardner's response and how he defused the situation by talking openly and directly to the union leaders and the disaffected workforce.

---

**Box 6.2    Stakeholder Management at Trans Hex Group**
*(See Box 4.2 for background)*

For about 13 years of his incarceration in Robben Island, Nelson Mandela shared his sentence with a fellow veteran of the war for black emancipation, Tokyo Sexwale. On his release from jail, Sexwale followed Mandela into political leadership in post-Apartheid South Africa. In 1998 he left public life for the

private sector where, encouraged by black empowerment legislation, he established Mvelaphanda Diamonds and targeted
Trans Hex Group (THG) for acquisition. In early 2000 he took
an 8% stake in THG and swiftly increased his stake.

When Calvyn Gardner was hired as a turnaround specialist in
September 2001 he faced a rapidly deteriorating situation. He
realised that for a successful turnaround he had to satisfy all key
stakeholder constituencies and not just the equity stakeholders
who had brought him in.

Gardner stresses that no turnaround strategy can succeed without buy-in, both from above, at Board level and below among
senior and middle management. After 35 days he submitted his
plan to the Board, who swiftly adopted it.

> *"It was only a skeleton, but it was a foundation. It was a team
> effort with the Board and by the end of the day we had a docu-
> ment that everyone signed off on. They (the Board) were part of
> the process. It was never a matter of them simply saying 'yes' or
> 'no'. It was impossible for this (turnaround) to have happened
> without the Board buying in."*

His strategy in place, Gardner then focused his efforts on developing lines of communication with his remote mine managers,
so that he might broadcast the strategy among them, win their
buy-in, and get feedback from them.

What was unique about the Trans Hex situation was the political and social environment in which the turnaround was taking
place. Soon after his arrival THG was hit by a union-backed
strike when negotiations stalled. The situation is described by
Calvyn Gardner as follows:

> *"There was an atmosphere of hate on both sides between man-
> agement and the workforce which had its roots in the apartheid
> system of the previous government. Very little had changed from
> a worker perspective since independence in 1994. Living con-
> ditions for the workers, in single hostel type accommodation,
> were extremely poor; catering and general hygiene of the hostel
> facilities were a disgrace. Family members lived long distances*

*from the workplaces and workers saw their families one weekend per month."*

*"Few people had received any new training resulting in no black people being promoted to more senior positions. Management was predominantly white and 95% of the white workers had their families accommodated at the mines, in free company housing. The human resource strategy was not in line with the Government's approach of fast track on-the-job training and creation of equity in the workplace. The labour turnover was high, as was the use of the disciplinary code (mainly used on black employees) resulting in a high proportion of dismissals."*

*"There was a shooting incident where workers fired on management and management returned fire, resulting in the police and army arriving at the mines. Offices, houses, buses and plants were burned and damaged. I flew to Johannesburg and had an emergency meeting with the President of the union, asking him to stop the violence and open the doors for dialogue. We discussed the position of Trans Hex for more than five hours, and we agreed that the current position needed radical change. I shared all the details of my financial plan with them – the first time the union had ever been treated in this way. A week later after our first meeting with the union's regional committee, they agreed to go back to work and to continue wage negotiations."*

*"I flew to the flagship operation Baken for a three-day visit. There was still much tension on site with little courtesy being given between workers and management. It was the first evening around 9pm that I decided to visit the hostel which is where most of the violence had started and where the main leaders of the workers were to be found. The visit completely surprised the hostel dwellers. I requested to visit the facility and was conducted on a full tour by the hostel leaders. All 300 hostel dwellers watched as I was offered food which I declined."*

*"I agreed that the facility was a disgrace and promised to upgrade starting immediately. I requested a hostel committee be established who would lead the upgrade and would liaise with mine management. I also informed them this would be the last time I would refuse food in the canteen and that the management*

*canteen would be closed and all mine personnel including myself would eat at this one facility."*

*"Within three months, a new kitchen and canteen was built, all dormitories upgraded, family accommodation built and a new entertainment area built. The walls were starting to come down and a new belief in the company started to take hold. The wage agreement was signed six weeks after the initial strike and no further strikes took place."*

Calvyn Gardner embraced the post-Apartheid focus on achieving black empowerment and ownership, appointing black managers at the top of the hierarchy at two of the mines. Rather than the engineers one typically finds in the role of mine manager, Gardner's managers came from a human resources background. They in turn worked to implement a broad "upliftment programme" aimed at improving opportunities for blacks and coloureds within Trans Hex. They introduced literacy and computer training programmes for workers previously denied such opportunity for education. These "Black Empowerment" efforts went well beyond those mandated by the South African government, and were tied in to the company's effort to build better relationships with the mining unions. Trans Hex reached out to the local communities in which they operated, providing educational opportunities for their schoolchildren, and opening an "internet café" at the mine, available to them without cost. It is hoped that these community-based efforts will help to ensure future availability of a local labour force that feels it benefits by working with Trans Hex.

Treating the workforce with respect, giving them an honest appraisal of the risks and challenges, and keeping them informed about developments within the turnaround process are practices adopted by good turnaround leaders. Being seen to deal fairly with the workforce is critical to earning their respect and maintaining their support:

*"When the decision was made to close the new plant, staff were told immediately, even though it was six months prior to the planned*

*closure. Job retraining was set up on site and competitors and others in the field were contacted to help find new jobs . . . no one likes redundancies but people got to air their concerns and they all felt it was a fair process."*

# Government

Government at all levels is more often a key stakeholder in turnaround situations than is commonly realised – leaving aside their potential role as customers. They may have an economic interest as shareholders or financiers – as they did in Railtrack; a legal interest as regulators or a political interest, either where there is a massive corporate scandal as with Enron in the USA or Parmalat in Italy or where there are potential political consequences, as in the failure of the car manufacturer Rover shortly before the 2005 General Election in the UK.

The rescue of the Royal Opera House (Covent Garden) provides an interesting example of the turnaround leader's critical interaction with government, in order to achieve a turnaround solution. In 2000, the Royal Opera House was in a major financial crisis since, although money had been raised to build a magnificent new Opera House, there was a significant operating deficit and no means of bridging it without external funding, even if all performances were sold out and private donations were maintained at historic levels. A turnaround executive, Pelham Allen, had been appointed as acting chief executive and he, together with the chairman, Sir Colin Southgate, had to make it clear that the Opera House would be completely closed down unless the government significantly increased funding for operational costs. A compromise was finally reached whereby the Opera House would provide two-thirds of the opera for two-thirds of the funds.

At the British Library the new management team discovered that some key stakeholders in government had not been visited for five years. They found that officials at the Ministry of Science and Technology, a key stakeholder, were not well acquainted with the Library; and that another stakeholder group, Members of Parliament, were also badly informed. The new chief executive and her team embarked on a mission to rebuild stakeholder confidence through a process of open consultation, communication and the provision of reliable information. This process was helped by the appointment of a new director of Strategic Marketing and Communication whose role included stakeholder management. The subsequent appointment of a new chairman, Lord Eatwell, in September 2001 also helped to rebuild government relationships.

In some industries, regulators can be crucial stakeholders and can determine if a company will survive. For example, the holiday company My Travel, which underwent a restructuring in 2004–5, publicly raised concerns that the Civil Aviation Authority might revoke its company's licence to trade if the restructuring process continued to drag on. It was generally perceived that management sought to use this "threat" to put pressure on the convertible bondholders, who were contesting the terms of the deal. Nonetheless, had the CAA revoked My Travel's licence due to its financial instability, it would have been forced to cease trading immediately and all hope of a successful turnaround would have ended.

## The Board of Directors

Turnaround executives appear to have widely different views about the role played by Boards in distressed companies. Some see them as irrelevant at best or an obstacle at worst – since they had presided over the downfall of the business – and may seek to "work around" or even remove the Board. Others consider that having the Board's support is crucial to the success of a turnaround. This depends to a certain extent on whether it is a public or a private company and where the power lies between debtor and creditor. The following quotations from leading practitioners illustrate the diversity of their views:

> "I generally ignore the Board . . . by the time I arrive the power is with the creditors."

> "The role of the Board is very limited, especially in public companies. They have slow decision-making processes, they find it difficult to make things happen fast . . . they are a nuisance."

> "I work with the Board as far as possible but I usually change them all at any rate."

*"I will not take on an assignment unless it is unanimously approved by the Board."*

It is critical that the Board is at the very least neutral (or neutered!) and does not overtly or covertly undermine the turnaround leader's efforts. The turnaround leader will not "play politics" with the Board and will usually resign if he or she cannot get the Board to support the turnaround plan.

## Financial Analysts

In a public company the turnaround leader cannot ignore financial analysts. The turnaround leader who has not been in such a situation before needs to tread carefully and take expert advice, typically from a City PR firm in the case of a high-profile or public company. The new turnaround leader needs to "buy time" with the analysts and should never be "bounced" into promising too much – for example, giving a profit forecast – in the early months. There is usually a lag in analysts' perceptions and coverage of the company during a turnaround since they are only persuaded by financial results. However, they are never satisfied and the turnaround leader must be very careful not to over-promise.

## The Press

Most turnaround professionals like to operate as discreetly as possible and find that the press are rarely a help. Most say they go out of their way to avoid high-profile press interviews and articles. However, some large turnarounds are inevitably high profile because they make a good story – particularly High Street names, and companies that are well known to nearly everybody, such as Marks & Spencer and Sainsburys. In these situations the turnaround leader cannot completely ignore the press. Commenting on this, one well-known turnaround leader said:

*"If you can't ignore them (the press) make sure you use them to your advantage . . . be very selective in who you talk to."*

Again, the support of experienced PR professionals can be critical in putting across the message with as much positive "spin" as the leader feels is appropriate, consistent with the ongoing requirement to under-promise and over-deliver. Employees, customers and suppliers will read and be influenced by press coverage; while silence is preferable, managing the press is increasingly a requirement in high-profile restructuring situations.

# No Magic Formula

In chapter 4 we discussed how the turnaround leader needs to exhibit the 3Cs – credibility, clarity and courage – if he or she is to "grab hold" of the business. This applies equally to dealing with external stakeholders:

> *"One has to establish a common level of trust with all the key stakeholders fast . . . this is why track record and credibility are so important for a turnaround leader."*

The essence of providing leadership to the stakeholder management process during turnaround is well summarised by one turnaround executive as follows:

> *"Leadership should focus on keeping all partners engaged in the process while at the same time not over-promising. Communication is the key . . . keep talking to people, keep them in the loop."*

Finally, a word of warning. Communicating with all interested stakeholders can be very time consuming and their attitude(s) can change rapidly:

> *"While turnaround might be possible in the morning, by afternoon the situation may have changed."*

In summary, the following rules are applied by all successful turnaround leaders in managing their stakeholders:

- Be open – be honest.
- Think straight and talk straight.

- Do your homework to ensure that you are communicating high-quality information.

- Negotiate effectively.

- Manage both stakeholders' perceptions and expectations.

- Understand the personal agendas of the stakeholder representatives as well as their corporate or institutional agenda.

- And above all COMMUNICATE WITH CLARITY to the right degree.

Stakeholder management is critical for any leader in any situation. Not only is it the "engine oil" that allows the turnaround to proceed, but if it is done well it provides an umbrella for the management team, shielding them from stakeholder pressures and allowing them to focus on fixing the problems the company faces.

# 7

# Strategic Focus

IN OUR EARLIER BOOK, *CORPORATE TURNAROUND*, WE IDENTIFIED 10 principles for developing corporate and business unit strategies in a turnaround.

- *Tackle the "where" and "how"* – the need to articulate a vision for the organisation and how it will be achieved.

- *Sell into a need* – the strategy must be built around a customer value proposition that not only meets the needs of customers but does it at least as well as competitors.

- *Maximise strengths* – identifying and building fast on the company's strengths is critical to success.

- *Business focus* – almost every successful turnaround requires the firm to develop a focused strategy which implies withdrawing from industry sectors, product/market segments or selected activities in the value chain.

- *Be radical* – drastic action is usually required to turn around a company in trouble.

- *Stretch but not too much* – the stretch must be enough to make turnaround a better option than sale or liquidation but be credible in light of the company's strengths and weaknesses.

- *Cash is king* – the strategy must fit the financial constraints so strategies that use cash are not usually feasible in the short term.

- *Learn to walk before learning to run* – in the early stages of a turnaround, stabilisation is the prime objective, so new strategies often have to wait until recovery is underway.

- *Urgency and action bias* – strategic analysis must be completed quickly and lead to immediate action.

- *Focus on key strategic issues* – the turnaround leader has to "nail" the three or four critical issues and not worry about the others.

This chapter explains how turnaround leaders achieve strategic focus using many of the principles outlined above. Our research shows that strategic focus is a fundamental step towards achieving a sustainable turnaround and must usually be implemented before any growth strategies are considered. There are examples of companies in trouble, such as Worldcom (now renamed MCI) where growth was an immediate and viable option, but for companies in mature industries – where a lot of turnarounds are to be found – fundamental competitive weaknesses cannot be eradicated without adopting a more focused strategy.

Not all individuals who claim to be turnaround practitioners have the capability or desire to become involved in developing and implementing new strategies. As we described in chapter 1, some are primarily crisis stabilisation experts. Even among the turnaround advisers we see this distinction. Perspectives on turnaround strategy from company doctors and advisors vary from "I don't get involved in this" (the quick fix crisis stabiliser) to "this is the most important element in a turnaround". By the time crisis stabilisation is completed, a good turnaround leader should have a good strategic understanding of the business and be in a position to lead a strategy formulation process to create real value for stakeholders.

# Divestment

The job of leading the turnaround of a multi-business corporation nearly always involves choosing one (or more) core businesses to focus on and exiting the remainder. Earlier research by one of the authors showed that divestment is the single most common cash-generating strategy used by UK public companies in trouble. A divestment programme is sometimes referred to as corporate restructuring (although we prefer not to use that term since it is often confused with financial restructuring).

Some turnaround practitioners argue that divestment is a straight-forward management process, albeit time consuming, which can be project managed from the preparation of the sale memorandum through to the handover to the new buyer(s). While strong project management skills are essential, good leadership skills are also necessary if the troubled company is to maximise the sale proceeds of its divestment programme, do it quickly, and implement all the other critical aspects of its turnaround plan.

In some situations, implementing the divestment programme is the single most important aspect of the turnaround. When Sir Christopher Bland was appointed Chairman of British Telecom in 2001, he made a list of 10 things he had to achieve in the first 12 months, six of which involved divesting businesses to reduce the crippling corporate debt which then amounted to £30 billion, accruing interest charges of £1 million per day. Box 7.1 describes what happened at British Telecom over the 12-month period.

---

### Box 7.1    Divestment at British Telecom

When Sir Christopher Bland was appointed chairman of BT in May 2001, BT's borrowings were £30 billion and he did not have a lot of choice other than to lead a divestment programme. Indeed it was made clear to him by the key financial stakeholders that he could only become chairman if he agreed to the demerger of the mobile business $mmO_2$ (previously Cellnet). He wanted three months to review the decision but was given three days, and on balance he thought it was the right thing to do. "It was the price of the rights issue", he says, "the biggest ever seen in the UK".

Within 10 months, BT had reduced its borrowings to under £15 billion, using a variety of cash-generating strategies, including a rights issue and significant disposals.

|                               | *Approx. proceeds* *(£billion)* |
| ----------------------------- | ------------------------------- |
| Rights issue                  | 6.0                             |
| Sale of YELL                  | 2.0                             |
| Sale of Japanese investments  | 3.3                             |

| Sale of Airtel (Spain) | 1.1 |
|---|---|
| Sale of other assets | 1.3 |
| Sale and leaseback of property | 2.4 |
| **Total:** | **16.1** |

Interestingly, Sir Peter Bonfield, the chief executive who had been instrumental in buying many of the businesses, was involved in the sale process and "some good prices" were obtained. At the same time BT unwound its joint venture agreement with AT&T (Concert), which was losing money at the rate of US$800 million per year.

In addition to dismantling the old BT corporate strategy and refocusing on the core landline business, Sir Christopher's other major achievement during the first year was to hire a new CEO, who started in January 2002. He says he started with a list (kept in his wallet) of 10 things he had to do in the first year and he achieved nine of them; only failing to sell BT's minority stake in the French mobile operator Cegetel.

The analysis to determine what businesses to divest is usually simplistic and pragmatic, loss-making businesses, businesses which require significant cash injections to prosper, and businesses unrelated to the "core" are usually the prime candidates. However, the need for a quick sale and the relatively weak negotiating position of the seller may mean that the company has to divest itself of some of its "crown jewels" (the good businesses it would really like to keep). Sometimes the turnaround leader is not even in control of the decision, as was the case at BT, where Sir Christopher Bland was offered the job on the condition that the mobile phone business mmO$_2$ was demerged.

By taking an active leadership role in the divestment process, the turnaround leader can inject urgency into the process and, more importantly, lead the negotiating process in order to extract maximum value from the purchaser. This may involve retaining key people (who would otherwise be let go) to manage the process or persuading, motivating and even coaching the management of the company being sold to help to sell the business. One company doctor who has worked on several divestment programmes says:

> *"I look for a buyer with an ego so as to obtain a significantly higher selling price. For example, in one turnaround, I was pressurised by the Board and the bank to fire the incumbent CEO, but I retained him for the purpose of selling the heavily loss making 'core' business. I knew that this individual had convinced the banks to invest time and time again. He understood the company and how to package and present the company in its best possible light to another provider of capital (the prospective purchaser)."*

Maintaining the commitment of employees during divestment can be partly achieved through the use of financial incentives, but this alone is insufficient. At the family-owned soft drinks business mentioned in Chapter 3, David James started on a turnaround process but after three months he decided he needed to sell all the businesses, and not just the non-core assets (see Box 7.2). He used financial incentives but perhaps more importantly he motivated employees to feel a sense of responsibility for successful completion of the break-up process. What was noticeable in this situation was a respect for the contribution of employees at all levels, trust in employees to get the job done, and effective two-way communication of what was expected from all parties involved.

---

**Box 7.2   Breaking up a Family-Owned Soft Drinks Business**

About three months after David James and his team had taken control of the business, it became apparent that the company's over-investment in carbonated drink manufacturing, combined with increasing competition in this segment of the business, meant that the goal had to change from potential turnaround to workout. The profitable portions of the business had to be sold to pay back the liabilities. However, this required separating out and streamlining the operational aspects of the different business units so that they could be sold off individually. The whole process would take about two years.

Leadership at this stage was primarily focused on choosing senior managers that could contribute to the sale value of the businesses in question. This required a quick assessment to determine who could contribute to current business needs. The new management team quickly identified existing talent within the company and promoted them to key roles, while mentoring and managing as opposed to looking outside their organisation for new talent.

The first assets to be sold were non-core, such as a Mews House in London, the plastic moulding division of the engineering business and the old manufacturing facility, which was sold to a government backed regeneration group for a good price. The total proceeds were about £6 million, £4 million of which was returned to the banks and £2 million retained for working capital.

The water company was valued at only c. £8 million in a break-up situation, but the turnaround team felt this was too low. On investigation it was discovered that a similar company had recently been sold for £20 million. In addition, the Group had been actively pursuing the development of a new carbonated drink product, as a brand extension to its well-recognised mineral water brands. Over a six-month period this new product was rushed to market. The carbonated fruit drink had promising sales and was deemed to have significant growth potential. Soon after this a buyer was found for £20 million.

After some negotiation, and clearance through the Office of Fair Trading, the squash concentrate business was sold to a competitor. The sale included all contracts as well as the equipment from the new plant. However, the sale was also contingent on the condition that enough product was stockpiled to fill customer demand during the estimated three months it would take to disassemble the manufacturing equipment from the existing factory and reassemble it at the purchaser's new plant. To meet this requirement, the Group had to increase capacity utilisation at the current facility from a previous best of less than 50% to a sustained level of above 60%. Achieving this required setting up significant incentive schemes for staff. When the decision was made to close the new plant, staff were told immediately even though it was six months prior to closure. Job retraining was set up on site and competitors and local companies were contacted to help to find new jobs for employees.

Accepting the reality early in the process that turnaround was not a viable option, the company operated for two additional years and paid off all its creditors in full. By October 1999, one year after the turnaround team's arrival, over half the bank debt had been repaid. In the end about £52 million was generated of which £39 million principal was returned to the banks plus £5 million interest with the remainder being used to fund the attempted turnaround, legal fees, employee bonuses and operating costs.

In our view, the turnaround was a success. When the team entered the company, financial distress threatened the immediate closure of the firm. When the team finished their job, banks, creditors and employees had all received promised payments, and viable business units remained in operation albeit under different ownership.

The divestment process at the company was made all the more difficult by the need to separate the product lines into standalone operating units before sale – each with senior management capable of running the business without the decision making control previously exercised by the family owners. While he might not have had another option – because it is very difficult to attract good people to a troubled business that you are about to sell – David James used individuals within the group to manage these teams.

## Strategic Vision

During the crisis stabilisation phase, the vision is usually short term and can be summed up in one word: "survival". However, the turnaround leader soon finds it necessary to articulate something more about the company's future direction. Strategic leadership, as it is known in the management literature, requires the leader to articulate a view about the future size and scope of the company - what businesses or product/market segments the firm plans to focus on and how it plans to differentiate itself in its market(s).

Not all turnaround leaders feel confident about doing this or believe it is part of their job, even though they may exhibit strong leadership characteristics during crisis stabilisation. Even those that do believe in strategic refocusing often approach the process from an analytical and management perspective rather than leading by articulating a vision. The transient nature of turnaround leadership means that many feel that the ongoing management of the company should decide where the company goes in the longer term.

While this approach is shared by many turnaround practitioners – particularly those who focus on the stabilisation phase of turnaround – there are an increasing number of company doctors who believe it is critical to develop and communicate a vision of the future as soon as they have a good feel for the company and the industry in which they are working. The vast majority of employees want to be led and want to know where they are going. One turnaround executive with a military background told us:

*"In a turnaround people need to see a long-term picture. I can easily see the big picture, frame it for the organisation, and finally communicate it simply. I try to communicate this picture to management and employees in the very early days. I try to organise a 'post-it' session within three to four days which captures the major issues and opportunities from which I develop the big picture."*

The more analytically trained turnaround leaders, whether they be company doctors, venture capitalists or advisers, are often able to articulate a medium term vision (say up to three years hence) for the distressed firm.

Raoul Hughes, of the venture capital company Bridgepoint, provides an interesting example. Bridgepoint having taken an equity position in an integreted UK package holiday operator that was near insolvency, was faced with a reinvestment decision. Bridgepoint's analysis showed that the company was not viable in the long run as a standalone business because it had few assets and there were high ongoing bonding requirements to stay afloat. A detailed industry analysis helped Hughes and his team to develop a view about industry consolidation; and a "vision" that this company could have significant value for one of the bigger competitors as it would bring a good revenue stream with little incremental investment or additional overhead requirement. This proved to be the case as it subsequently sold for a significant premium on investors' monies.

At Lee Cooper, Paul Hick developed a strategic vision for the company as soon as he had completed a 30-day diagnostic review, and thus provided the framework for the turnaround (see Box 7.3). The vision and the objectives that emanated from it, were communicated to all staff, and everyone in the organisation was expected to contribute towards achieving the vision. Paul then encouraged teamwork around each of the key objectives and empowered the teams – undoubtedly under his guidance – to offer solutions.

---

**Box 7.3    Strategic Vision and Innovation at Lee Cooper**

From 1959 to 1994 Lee Cooper was a publicly quoted company and became the second largest jeans and casual apparel company in Europe. It had subsidiaries in France, Belgium, Germany and Switzerland, had licensing agreements in 27 countries, a factory in Tunisia and a logistics centre in France. In 1994 it was taken private by a venture capital firm and other investors. In 1998, with sales of £60 million and a further £60 million through licensing and profit of £6 million (as against a budget of £10 million), the key shareholders brought in Paul Hick as CEO to turn the business around and prepare it for sale. The banks were concerned about debt servicing and had already appointed a restructuring partner from an international accountancy firm. Paul Hick's in-depth review (undertaken after he arrived) included one-to-one meetings with 65 people, mostly middle managers in addition to the nine directors. After "listening to them" for 30 days coupled with his belief that they were the ones who really understood Lee Cooper's business and knew the solutions as well as the problems, he worked with them to define what the Lee Cooper of 2003 would look like in terms of brand, product innovation, supply chain, customer service, channels and resources. This process took about a month and was supplemented by Paul sifting through a large quantity of data provided to him by external and internal sources on market trends, competitors, sourcing costs and financial performance.

By the time Paul put his turnaround plan to the Board for their approval, he was asked to articulate his five-point vision.

• A European-focused sales and marketing led organisation.

• A leader in product innovation.

- World class manufacturing in Tunisia.

- Be a totally customer-focused organisation.

- Create a successful "Anglo-Latin" company culture to out-perform the European leader, Levi's (which tends to impose US values and ways on its organisation and customers).

Paul believed that building an Anglo-Latin culture involves taking the best of each culture and integrating them together: putting planning, discipline, innovation and organisation alongside fantastic creativity, style and superior commitment to delivery and implementation from the Latin side.

Paul set up teams to work on the key issues necessary to implement the vision. One such team, the marketing team, were tasked with addressing the brand image issue since Paul had learned that the Lee Cooper image in France was "something that farmers would wear" and that in the UK it was what "a father would wear" – and it was thus unappealing to the fashion-conscious younger age group that he wanted to target. Once he had identified the issues and agenda, the teams were empowered and encouraged to make their own decisions. The marketing team developed a new brand proposition: "built in performance for style and fun".

Throughout the turnaround Paul's leadership style encouraged teamwork especially among the many different nationalities that made up the company. The culture changed from being conservative, passive and change-resistant to one that was challenging, supportive, innovative and very results focused.

The starting point for the culture change was undoubtedly the strategic visioning exercise, and Paul instituted the following two informal tests to ensure that the vision (and subsequent objectives) was getting through to the lower level in the organisation:

- The "doorman/receptionist test" – the ability of staff at all levels to articulate the company's vision and objectives.

- The "Timberland test" – the ability to recreate a "Lee Cooper shopping experience" so that a customer who does not know

> about Lee Cooper will understand what the brand stands for simply by entering a Lee Cooper store.
>
> The company was sold in 2001 at an EBIT multiplier which was 50% higher than that of its sector at the time.

Neither Raoul Hughes nor Paul Hick in the examples given above had to spend most of their time on crisis stabilisation and stakeholder management. Immediate survival was not the issue. Therefore one could argue that they had the time to do the analysis from which their respective visions emerged. This is not always possible and it is often six or more months into a turnaround before the leader has "the luxury to think beyond the next 10 days". However, once the immediate crisis is stabilised, the need to think more strategically about the business will be there – and it may be at this time that the turnaround leader exits, and is replaced with a permanent CEO, perhaps with industry experience. There are, however, two schools of thought on this subject. Does one bring in an industry expert who knows the industry or an outsider who can bring fresh thinking to the strategy process?

Sometimes it is at this point in the turnaround process that there is a difference of opinion between the turnaround leader and one or more of his senior managers; for example, where the leader is in a chairman role with a CEO/MD who has been executing the day-to-day turnaround activities. This happened at Virgin Express, where the MD (who had industry experience) wanted to grow the company again after crisis stabilisation, whereas David Hoare, a turnaround expert who had been brought in as chairman, believed that further consolidation was more appropriate. The CEO was replaced, because unless the chairman and CEO share the same vision for the business, the management team and the rest of the organisation would be receiving mixed messages – a sure recipe for inaction and/or potential failure.

## Product Market Refocusing

At the operating company or business unit level of the organisation, a lot of classic managerial analysis is necessary to decide which products and customers to drop and the ones on which to focus. The turnaround leader must ensure that this analysis gets done either by the management team(s) or by advisers/consultants. He or she must have the management competence to know what analysis needs to be done, and must lead the process, and act decisively on the conclusions of the analysis. The process should be action-oriented, and avoid multiple iterations and over-complicated analyses. One experienced practitioner describes his pragmatic approach:

> *"Keep in mind that turnarounds should be a short term fix . . . so the refocusing you do is very basic. In one deal I am reducing the number of customers from 60 to 4 – that is the type of thing you focus on. The leadership you provide is one of guidance and you should make every thing very down to earth."*

When dealing with a single business or an operating company of a multi-business corporation, the starting point should always be to determine if the company is indeed a single strategic business unit or is actually a number of business units fused into a single organisational entity (see Box 7.4).

---

### Box 7.4    Separating the Business Units

Zenith* was an entrepreneurially owned stevedore and shipping company in the North of England backed by a venture capital company. The company was losing £0.5 million per year and although there was no immediate crisis the investors asked Tony McCann to work as Chairman alongside the entrepreneur and his managing director. One of his first tasks was to ask the Finance Director to draw up separate profit/loss and cash flow forecasts for what he saw as two distinct business units. He discovered that the shipping business was losing £5 million per year while the stevedore operations showed a profit of £4.5 million per year.

The managing director was told to sell the two ships they owned but resisted doing so. After three months he had not come close to a sale and was replaced. The ships were sold within months for £8 million in cash, which took a loss-making asset off the balance sheet and reassured the investors of the company's remaining viability and solvency. The stevedore operations were sold a year later for approximately £16 million.

* The company name has been disguised.

The majority of company doctors recognise the critical role of product/market refocusing; however, their degree of involvement in the decision-making process and implementation varies considerably, as is evidenced by the following comments:

*"Future strategy must be led by the parties in the company who have been identified as being passionate about the organisation. It is for these people to take their ideas and with their new found ability to act on them (provided by people like myself) to lead the organisation forward."*

*"Most of the managers with whom I work have a better knowledge of the business than I do. They must run the show and I try not to interfere. In this situation, leadership is the capability to step aside and look objectively at what is happening."*

*"This is a stage in the turnaround that the companies themselves have to manage. My role is to be the leader that initiates refocusing and keeps on pushing."*

*"Refocusing the business strategy is a critical part of my role."*

*"This is often the most important part of a turnaround. In almost all businesses there is a need to contract before you can grow."*

*"Once you've analysed the problem your job is to find the way out."*

*"In order to develop a strategy, I invested a lot of my personal time talking to customers directly and working with focus groups."*

*"I work closely with key customers so as to be able to better understand their specific needs for each of the company's products."*

The extent to which the turnaround leader gets involved in the detail of product and market strategies will understandably depend on the size of the company and the diversity of its product/market portfolio. Leaders with industry experience are clearly more likely to believe they can add more value to the strategy process than those from outside the industry.

With this spectrum of views, it is not surprising that the leadership style used to achieve strategic change varies from facilitation of the process at one end of the spectrum, to "selling a plan", which the company doctor has already decided, at the other. What all agree on, however, is that it is vital to obtain the ownership and commitment of the key managers that have to implement the plan, and it is vital to maintain control by monitoring the implementation process.

George Moore, a turnaround executive, says that once he has put together a team to undertake a turnaround, he leaves them to work out a plan of how to proceed:

*"They will provide a lot of the input, as they will have detailed knowledge of the business and its problems. I am only an outsider with little industry experience, so I see my role as that of the facilitator who draws the ideas out of the people and galvanises them into action. During this process I get them to state what needs doing, who will do it, and what the milestones are. It is important to have named individuals for each task so that there is ownership of each task. The process is ongoing and nothing is ever more than 10 days away."*

Nicholas Ward, another turnaround executive, stresses the same point when he says:

*"The final strategy and accompanying plan of action is a textbook in 'what', 'when' and 'how' – crafted with the contributions of the top team, so that commitment is explicit as we proceed to the implementation stage."*

He involves top management substantially in the process – not just in the creation of the strategy document but also in the administration of it through performance reviews and individual accountability:

*"It is an ongoing process with the business plan being constantly updated and modified. I try to act as a mentor to top managers – a*

*person to whom they can turn for advice and answers on unfamiliar
aspects of their work. I encourage senior executives to be open and
creative, within the bounds of the plan . . . but the risk stays with me
and that gives senior managers the confidence to achieve."*

One way of refocusing the business is to take management out of
their everyday roles and allow them time to concentrate on the wider
(strategic) issues. Several leaders we spoke to favoured using "away-
days" at external locations every quarter.

At one UK furniture manufacturer, we witnessed a turnaround CEO
surface resistance early on, when formulating a new detailed plan for
the business. He designed a process to solicit formal and informal
input across the company during the business plan brainstorming
phase, without fully divulging the details of what he had in mind.
This engaged staff but also allowed him to uncover potential areas
of resistance across the organisation before the plan was released.
Careful timing gave room for some of the early resistance to subside,
giving a higher chance of buy-in and commitment to the plan. This
process is illustrated in Figure 7.1

Involvement and participation in developing the new strategic focus
do not, however, fit every turnaround leader's style, as indicated by
the following quote:

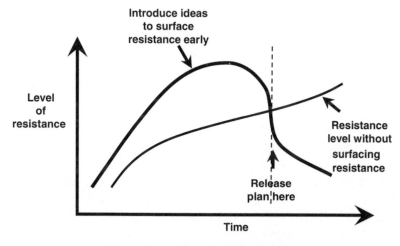

Figure 7.1   Timing and resistance

*"Once I have developed a plan I will hold discussions with manage-*
*ment to convince them that it is as much their plan as mine, effectively*
*forcing them to take ownership. It is much easier than you think. With*
*the staff I am not wrapped up in proving how smart I am . . . if you*
*drop an idea with the staff, they are highly suggestible . . . they end up*
*thinking it is their plan."*

Contrary to the notion that those that are "not with you" go immediately, this turnaround executive believes that this is the time (at
the beginning of strategic refocusing) to remove the doubters in the
management team:

*"Refocusing the company requires a spirit of positivism. With this in*
*place and the sources of negativity gone, you can 'sell' the plan to the*
*remaining managers."*

The need to obtain ownership and commitment of the key implementers – by whatever approach – clearly requires a somewhat different leadership style than that that may be necessary in the crisis phase
of a turnaround. We see autocratic leadership styles becoming more
collaborative. More support and encouragement, even coaching or
mentoring, is seen as appropriate by some company doctors. However, culture change is achieved only relatively slowly and most company doctors find that they need to remain fairly directive throughout
the refocusing phase, as strong control cannot be compromised, and
there is a danger that the organisation will revert quickly to its old
*modus operandi* and believe that the need for urgency has passed.

Box 7.5 describes how John Ensall developed a new strategy at Clares
Group by involving his business unit managing directors and gradually giving them more freedom as he became confident that they
could deliver the necessary results.

---

**Box 7.5    Refocusing the Business: Clares Group**

Clares Group manufactures specialist industrial components.
In 1997 it had a turnover of £46 million and a net loss of £5
million. With debts of over £23 million and a negative net worth,
the company was put into receivership in October 1997. John
Ensall was brought in by the receiver with another company
doctor, George Wardale, to stabilise the business and prepare

it for sale. Six months later the business was sold and John was asked to stay on as CEO, and rebuild the business.

Commenting on this transition John said:

*"As the cash crisis eased and trading improved . . . smiles came back on people's faces . . . managers began to gain more confidence as profitability improved and wanted to discuss how they could contribute towards the medium and longer term success of the business. I realised that my leadership style must change."*

John appointed five managing directors, each with his own management team, to oversee the five principal business units.

During the strategic redirection of the organisation, John, working collectively with his five managing directors, conducting a full strategic analysis (including SWOT, five forces and added-value analysis) for Clares five primary business units. Improving the profitability of each of these units resulted in an "eye-opening" experience for John as he realised that Clare's management did not know which of their products were the most profitable. For each of the five business units, a league table of every single product and service sold was created, showing key performance measurements such as turnover, gross margin, net profit margin, and contribution. Prior to showing them the results of the analysis, John asked his management to state their unit's most profitable products. More often than not, his managers selected the loss-making products as the ones they thought were the most profitable. The analysis resulted in the elimination of the bottom third of products from all league tables.

John explained that if customers insisted on purchasing these products they would have to pay three times the price. As a result, Clares produced a new catalogue and price list that had a massive positive impact on profitability.

As part of the business refocusing, and to emphasise a gradual change in his leadership style, John requested his five managing directors to prepare detailed three-year business plans showing the future direction of their business unit. Shortly thereafter, John held an off-site meeting for several days with his directors to review these plans. Together they rejected the plans; John and the directors then held a collective strategic session on the future of Clares, as a group. It was collectively decided that the new Clares Group strategy would require a move from being a manufacturing-focused company to a service-oriented company. The directors were requested to return to the business and rewrite their business plans in line with the new strategic direction. John was able to get his team to buy into this collective vision, which played a great part in its successful implementation and the subsequent movement of Clares from the refocusing phase into the growth phase.

In mid-1999 (close to one year out of receivership, and one month after the off-site meeting) the directors came back with revised business plans. Subsequently, John set individual targets for each of his five managing directors and further requested all employees to conduct an appraisal of their jobs in line with the new strategic direction. As the organisation progressed and people headed in the direction of the new strategy, John gradually released controls "as new management got up to speed". While he set levels for capital expenditure, revenue expenditure, employment levels, pay review and stock purchasing, he gave his five directors progressively more leeway to run their respective units by themselves. The rebuilding phase lasted for approximately 18 months. As his managers continued to meet their business plan objectives, more and more flexibility, and power were granted to them. John comments:

*"A good leader opens the minds of his managers to the future potential of the business, gives them support and encouragement, steering them without telling them what to do. It is essential to leverage good people to their maximum capabilities."*

During the rebuilding phase of the turnaround process, John's prior autocratic leadership style developed into more of a collaborative management style. Having put in a new structure and decision-making framework that was understandable to all employees, John became more of a facilitator and allowed managers to explore some of their own initiatives. However, more importantly, John recognised that he still had to remain relatively directive; strong controls could not be compromised as the business had yet to reach a position of sustainable recovery.

# Innovation

Strategic innovation has been more associated with corporate trans-formation and long-term thinking than with corporate turnaround. However, there are a number of examples where the turnaround leader has successfully fostered innovation as a key element of an overall turnaround strategy.

For distressed firms in high technology industries, continuing to invest in new product development is usually critical for success. At MCI (formerly Worldcom) re-energising product development and accelerating new product introductions were core elements of Michael Capellas' 100-day plan. The innovation was targeted on three areas of technology for application in focused market segments. Capellas' leadership style was built around one theme – the need to *"act with an outrageous sense of urgency"*.

Outside the high-technology area, one of the more impressive exam-ples of how innovation can be used in a turnaround is provided by Head Tyrolia Mares (HTM), the Austrian sports equipment manu-facturer bought from the Austrian government by the Swedish en-trepreneur, Johan Eliasch, in 1996. HTM was losing market share and "bucket loads" of money. Eliasch, in his role as chairman and majority shareholder, personally led a major product innovation ini-tiative with passion and enthusiasm. With little or no market research he developed the carving (hour-glass) ski, which has revolutionised skiing for beginners and intermediates alike. He later did this a second time with the introduction of the titanium tennis racket. Box 7.6 provides a synopsis of the turnaround at HTM.

---

**Box 7.6   Innovation at Head Tyrolia Mares**

After acquiring Head Tyrolia Mares from the (then) government-owned tobacco monopoly in 1995, Johan Eliasch, a Swedish entrepreneur, focused on cash management and re-structuring manufacturing to reduce the cost base:

> *"We had figured out a strategy that was really very simple. It was to cut down, to define the core businesses and focus on them. If anything did not fit the description we closed it."*

The main actions taken in the first year included:

- Reduced headcount by 30%, including 500 manufacturing and 400 administrative staff.

- Streamlined management by eliminating an entire layer of senior management.

- Initiated an immediate creditor standstill.

- Negotiated with the banks a substantial interest rate and debt waiver.

- Discontinued the loss-making US sportswear and distribution businesses and golf operation.

- Improved product mix in terms of SKU reduction, pricing levels, and elimination of self-competition, e.g. Tyrolia skis and boots

- Reworked the manufacturing capacity to adapt to reduced volumes.

- Reduced manufacturing costs through automation and increased productivity.

- Reduced fixed costs by streamlining sales and administrative functions.

- Improved financial controls and modernised MIS and IT systems.

- Liquidated non-core assets (US real estate and non-core inventories).

- Improved co-ordination of group activities.

- Relocated labour-intensive processes from Austria and Italy to the Far East (lower end rackets), Estonia (ski boots and diving equipment) and the Czech Republic (finishing and stringing rackets).

When asked how his perception of the key strategy decisions evolved, he said:

> *"The most important thing was that here was a company that was fighting... it had the right spirit and wanted to survive.*

> *Don't forget... it has to come from within. The guy leading the turnaround is the agent for change and has to lead people in the same direction."*

Within the divisions, research and development was "very perfunctory and not very innovative" – as is common in distressed firms in mature industries. However, due to Johan Eliasch's passion for sport and new ideas, innovation became a critical component of the turnaround:

> *"There was no radical change in the budget but we changed the culture to make people come up with ideas. We refocused on innovation, ideas... simple ones. I said almost immediately 'lets do a titanium tennis racket'... simple, light powerful. Gradually we made a product that made a real difference. They (the staff) needed to get out there, meet the customers, see what's happening at universities. Everyone... the entire company became part of R&D."*

Between 1995 and 1998 HTM launched titanium tennis rackets, carving skis and a revolutionary integrated dive system. According to Eliasch:

> *"These (innovations) were the basic reasons for HTM's turnaround. Titanium rackets changed the tennis industry and carving skis changed skiing."*

From a loss of $143 million on revenues of $400 million in 1995, profits were $7 million on revenues of $305 million in 1998. The company was floated on NASDAQ in 1999.

At Lee Cooper, the branded jeans manufacturer, Paul Hick was brought in as CEO in September 1998 by the venture capital shareholders. As part of his initial diagnostic review, he found that designers *"designed what they wanted to with virtually no attention to the consumer"*. He believed strongly that product innovation was critical in repositioning the Lee Cooper brand ("Built-in performance with style and fun"), and he challenged individuals to innovate when they said they could not do so. New products such as reversible jeans and waterproof jeans were developed by the incumbent design team, which not only typified the rejuvenated creativity of Lee Cooper but also allowed the brand to gain much needed publicity (see Box 7.3).

It is clear that middle management need the support of the leader in order to innovate. Johan Eliasch's direct involvement in product innovation, particularly in a company the size of HTM, is highly unusual. In most situations the leader sets the direction and then encourages middle management to drive the innovation process forward. Thus at the soft drinks company, (see Box 7.2), even though the company was being sold off business unit by business unit, the sales value of the spring water division was enhanced by bringing new products to market quickly. These products had been in the development pipeline for a long time but the new leadership made it very clear to the organisation that it was open to new ideas, and thereby unlocked value from within the company.

# Investment

Major investment in new products and/or markets is not a common turnaround strategy due to financial and time constraints, but from time to time one sees such a bold move. One example is provided by Carlos Ghosn at Nissan. In November 2000, 20 months after Renault took a stake in Nissan and Ghosn was appointed CEO to save the struggling company, Ghosn decided to invest $1.43 billion in a new manufacturing plant in the USA. This was based on his belief that a US production base would allow Nissan to build more models and target alternative segments in the US markets. At this stage Nissan had yet to show that it had turned around, but Ghosn took a calculated risk:

> *"There are moments when you have to make bold decisions. Our debt was high, we had no profit – just a sense that things would be under control. At the time people followed me more by discipline than conviction. Now everybody says it was obviously the right decision, but the challenge was to take the decision so early in the process. We could have waited another year, maybe two, before we had to make an investment, but we would have lost a lot of time."*

---

\* Quoted from *Independent on Sunday*, 18 May 2003.

Some bold strategic steps can lead to disaster as occurred when Ann Iverson – one of the many chief executives brought in to rescue Laura Ashley – decided that the "answer" to the retailer's problems were to open large stores in North America. Within two years Laura Ashley's US operation was losing £20 million on sales of £80 million.

Turnaround leaders who take such bold decisions either blight their reputations and risk ending their careers or are seen (subsequently) as far-sighted heroes. In reality, even the "heroes" are usually less certain of success than hindsight would suggest. As Carlos Ghosn said:

> *"The most difficult part is when you see something other people don't see and you can't back it by evidence. You question yourself: 'Am I doing the right thing? Am I going in the right direction?'"** 

Few turnaround leaders we know will go so far, but successful leaders are inclined to take more action rather than less and to refocus the company's strategy based on instinct and experience as much as on hard evidence and analysis.

# 8

# Changing Critical Business Processes

THE FOLLOWING IS PROBABLY THE MOST COMMON VIEW among turnaround professionals:

*"I prefer to secure talented managers who can implement the critical process improvements."*

However, just as with strategic refocusing (in the previous chapter) there is a full spectrum of views from *"I don't really do that sort of thing... I am not a detail person"* to *"I get heavily involved in this area because it is crucial to a sustainable turnaround"*.

## Identifying Critical Improvements

Turnarounds focus on a few critical processes that need fixing quickly and in which change can be implemented quickly. They are the ones that are likely to have a big impact on cutting costs, reducing working capital, improving quality or improving customer responsiveness. As David Hoare says:

*"The focus should be on processes that stand out in the diagnostic phase and are important to the stabilisation of the company."*

The diagnostic phase will often show a breakdown or malfunction of key processes; however, some of these may be expensive and time consuming to rectify, particularly where new or substantially modified IT systems are required (as is often the case with customer relationship management systems, for example). It is therefore important in the early stages of the turnaround, that the turnaround leader prioritises the big impact problem areas.

In many turnarounds, the lack of good-quality management information is the key priority area. This was the case at Target Express (see Box 3.2) where the financial controls and IT systems prevented new management from finding out what the real problem was. Sometimes basic processes such as invoicing systems are totally inadequate – as Jon Moulton found at Cedar – where he was quickly able to realise substantial cash when he discovered that the company had not invoiced many of its customers!

Outside the information area, improvements to procurement and production processes are likely to have the biggest short-term benefit, since demand-generating processes (sales and new product development, for example), while necessary in the medium term, tend to provide little in the way of short-term benefits. However, each situation is different and it may be a single process that is the root cause of the turnaround crisis. A business-to-business (B2B) courier company where Tony McCann was appointed as CEO, is just such an example – see Box 8.1.

---

**Box 8.1    Critical Process Improvement at B2B Courier**

B2B Courier was a company with sales in excess of £ 100 million which had been bought by a venture capital company in a highly leveraged transaction. Profit expectations were in the region of £ 10–12 million pre-tax but in reality were nearer £ 1.5 million. Under pressure from the venture capital company, costs had been cut which had destroyed the fundamental processes underlying the business model.

At the heart of the problem was a decision to eliminate a front end computer system costing £ 0.5 million that determined which letters they could accept for delivery, based on their couriers' locations. The result was that they were collecting mail they could not deliver. As the volume of undelivered mail grew, they sent it by Royal Mail, first class. They later reduced this to second class which took 5–6 days, cost £1.5 million and generated enormous complaints from customers who were paying to have next day delivery before 9 am! This resulted in the company building up a customer service team of 70 people to handle complaints. The total cost of the inefficiency was £5 million compared to the initial cost saving of £0.5 million.

Within two weeks of arriving the company doctor, Tony McCann, had solved the problem. The system was re-instated and within weeks the customer complaints team was disbanded. In the first year pre-tax profits returned to £6 million.

The experienced turnaround professional does not make unnecessary changes as it is all too easy for chaos to ensue, as one practitioner describes:

*"I was in a situation where my predecessor had restructured the entire financial reporting process resulting in accountancy chaos and lack of responsibility. Meanwhile the company still had no budgets or benchmarks that would allow them to measure progress against a baseline. You have to keep simplicity and clarity."*

# Management Information

The management information system (MIS) is the one area where the turnaround professional is most likely to be involved in process improvements. At Stormgard Plc, a textile company where the central accountancy system collapsed without any back-up, the chief accountant had a heart attack and a review of inventories showed a need for a £25 million write off. George Moore had to lead people through a reorganisation of reporting and control systems, at the same time as overseeing the recreation of 10 months of accounts. Advisers are also likely to get involved in this work and sometimes it is their major contribution if their role is completed – as it usually is – prior to a completion of the turnaround.

In leading process improvement in this area, turnaround leaders recognise that the existing finance director is almost inevitably not the right person to change the system. If he or she was, it would have been done earlier! While a new finance director might often be given the task of developing a new management information system, many finance directors, particularly in smaller companies, will not have the experience or resources necessary to do this:

> *"The first step is usually to take it [management information] away from the finance director whose responsibility it was and who had done nothing about it. . . . If the managing director is going to stay I will ask him to get to grips with management information. This uses the MD in a cross-functional way and gives him an opportunity to get closer to the business levers."*

## Leadership, Management or Both?

The role of the turnaround leader is to identify and prioritise critical process initiatives, initiate action and monitor their achievement. How hands-on they are will depend on their own experience, preferences and industry knowledge and the management resources at their disposal. Management skills of analysing, planning, organising and controlling are paramount as prerequisite for successful process improvement. The view of most company doctors is that this work is better carried out by operational managers who know the industry and/or "have done it before".

The following view is typical of many turnaround leaders:

> *"When it comes to restructuring or changing processes, ask the guys on the shop floor what should be done. If you need to get rid of a machine get them to decide which one . . . they have then made the decision and will make it work. They know more than someone like me who has just walked in and never used the machines. . . . Most of the time someone in the organisation has a solution or will be able to work out a way to solve problems."*

Pippa Wicks of AlixPartners, who is a former Group Finance Director of Courtaulds, says she likes to identify specific individuals who can "manage" the various workstreams (tasks) associated with process change. This does not mean that the turnaround leader abrogates responsibility, as the following comments from two turnaround professionals indicates:

> "I am not involved unless the process improvement is critical but if it is, it is then part of the business plan which is implemented through performance reviews and individual accountability."

> "I let the operational experts do their job. My role is to understand the overall picture, ensure the details are correct and challenge the assumptions. I delegate but remain in control."

Some turnaround leaders get heavily involved in the detail of process improvements, partly because they think it is important and partly because they like it:

> "I work closely with key customers to better understand their specific needs for each product and their frustrations in the purchasing process. I replicate this process with suppliers . . . "

Just how involved the leader becomes in the management process depends on the quality of the management team. Are they competent individuals to whom the turnaround leader can delegate, and, if not, can they be trained? Implementing critical process improvements means driving change rapidly through the organisation.

One experienced practitioner, who spent 20 years with GEC before becoming a turnaround specialist, believes that the biggest leadership challenges of the turnaround process are during process improvements.

> "This is the time individuals rebel against new processes and new job descriptions. It is usually the most painful time for the company as well: not only do undiscovered bombs explode but the financial position often gets worse before it gets better. The most important skill in leading this step of the turnaround is communication."

Employees need to be shown why the new methods and ideas are crucial and be persuaded to adopt them. Entirely new ways of doing business may have to be learned. Successful change management is

what delivers the results, as occurred at Exide Batteries where Lisa
Donahue implemented a team leadership programme with dramatic
results (see Box 8.2).

---

**Box 8.2    Exide Batteries**

Exide Technologies is the leading global manufacturer of industrial and automotive batteries, with nearly 20,000 employees, $2.5 billion in sales and vertically integrated operations in
89 countries. In 2000/2001, Exide ran into financial difficulties, as a result of its debt-financed global acquisition strategy,
inadequate integration of acquisitions and a downturn in automotive demand. By April 2002, its leverage (debt/EBITDA)
was close to 16 times and Exide filed for "Chapter 11" protection in the US courts. Lisa Donohue of AlixPartners, the
turnaround and performance improvement specialists, was appointed as Chief Restructuring Officer and Chief Financial Officer to Exide, charged with developing and implementing a
viable recovery strategy to take the business out of bankruptcy.
With the whole-hearted support of the CEO and Board, Lisa
led a global programme to improve financial performance.

At the heart of the recovery plan was **EXCELL** (Exide's
Customer-focused Excellence Lean Leadership). Exide did
not have the time or resources to reinvent the wheel but
synthesised many long-established performance improvement
methodologies such as Six Sigma and Kaizen, to create a set of
best practices in lean management while enhancing its sourcing
and distribution capability. The leadership team set audacious
goals – to launch EXCELL in 62 facilities world wide – and
communicated these through three simple targets:

1. To double output per individual and square foot at every
   plant, recycling centre and distribution facility.

2. To reduce the cost of quality by half.

3. To instil teamwork around the group.

Lisa selected a group of "Lean Leaders" or project managers
and established them as a "Center of Excellence". Lisa

deliberately chose leaders from within the business rather than outside consultants, in order to embed ownership within the organisation – this process "was invented here". The task of the "Lean Leaders" was to provide training and coaching around the group and to monitor progress. Measuring results was key to driving implementation and 10 key performance indicators were established, covering all aspects of the supply chain, including health and safety metrics. Five levels of certification for individual plants or facilities were established. The basic level was designed to be easily achievable, in order to demonstrate value quickly and get early buy-in; at the highest level, "stretch" targets were set including zero waste, 100% on-time delivery, zero accidents and zero defects. As a result of the EXCELL programme, WIP was cut by 30–40%, raw material levels by 61% and purchasing savings of $50 million per annum generated.

Throughout the process, Lisa had to ensure that she retained commitment to the changes, from Board level through to the shop floor. Communication was critical and was reinforced with incentive schemes that paid out generous bonuses if certain measurable milestones were reached. In addition, a discretionary bonus pool was established with beneficiaries nominated by their colleagues, which fostered enhanced team working and co-operation. As well as rewarding success, Lisa took tough action against those who impeded progress, removing the entire Board of an overseas subsidiary when they wouldn't approve the necessary changes.

Two years and a day after it had filed under "Chapter 11", Exide's Plan of Reorganisation was confirmed in the US Bankruptcy Court and it emerged with a substantial reduction in its gearing and greatly enhanced cash-generating capability.

Many competent managers may not have the leadership characteristics required for successful change management. If this is the case, the turnaround leader may need to provide the visible leadership, passion and commitment necessary to drive performance improvement. When changing the top team (see Chapter 4) the turnaround leader will ideally be looking for individuals with both management and leadership skills, but too often they end up with managers. Even then the good turnaround leader may get involved in the management detail to ensure that he or she has confidence in the actions that are being taken. Really competent turnaround leaders appear to have the ability to view the big picture and dive into the detail simultaneously.

In some industries – retailing is a good example – critical process improvements are usually at the core of any turnaround effort. At Marks & Spencer, the priority for Stuart Rose is to improve the product line and improve the efficiency of the supply chain in the core business area. Divestment and refocusing can buy time in the short term but the turnaround will not be considered successful until the core business is thriving. The same is true at Sainsburys in the food supermarket business.

What is required to succeed in these situations? Some of it is hard management analysis, which one can argue does not require industry experience, but more important are a refined intuition and a "hands-on" management style, typified by the following comment:

> *"I walk around the company to observe the critical processes and identify those that are not performing. . . . I do not have to rely on (dodgy) management reports that might not be accurate."*

## Empowerment or Discipline?

Implementing critical process improvements, particularly in the operational areas of the business, is likely to impact large numbers of people; and therefore the way in which it is carried out plays a big role in driving organisational change. While this is the topic of the next chapter the experienced turnaround leader knows that achieving some quick process improvement wins can kick-start the organisational change process.

Many of the turnaround professionals with whom we talked mentioned the need to empower or enable their employees to achieve change. Part of this is for the reasons we have already discussed – that the employees inside the company have the detailed knowledge and usually the answers – but part is due to the sheer scale of the change task. The sheer breadth of the business and the number of issues that the turnaround leader has to deal with are so great that he or she often has to lead from a background role, providing resources and pushing people to achieve change. However to undertake the change process the turnaround leader often has to do something symbolic to start the process. Taking a sledge hammer to the company's products, in full view of the workforce, at the start of a programme to improve product quality – a story one has heard a number of times – is typical of such a symbolic move. Box 8.3 describes the turnaround of a major engineering project and shows the power of symbolism at work on "Train 18". This is also an interesting example because it shows how the turnaround leader looked outside the organisation for answers to difficult process improvement issues.

---

### Box 8.3    Train 18

John Adkins led the turnaround of a major engineering contract. Although this was a project rather than a whole-company turnaround, John's leadership approach is relevant to many turnaround situations, particularly in the areas of critical process improvement and organisational change

John's employer was an Anglo-French entity that had contracted, through a subsidiary, to manufacture and deliver 165 new trains as part of a high-profile, government-sponsored infrastructure project. The total contract value was over £600 million, with a penalty of up to £100 million for late delivery. When John arrived the company was over a year behind schedule and had significant quality problems – in fact, all 17 of the trains it had delivered so far had been rejected. The customer was furious and had given the contractor an eight-week deadline to deliver train number 18 – without faults. The parent company had strongly held views as to the cause of the problem – " the assembly line is out of control" – and John's remit was to "fix it".

John quickly identified the true root cause; the design department continued to modify the design and specification of the trains throughout the manufacturing and assembly process, causing disruption and delay in production and delivery. This was exacerbated by a matrix organisation structure with a "Project Director" who was notionally in charge but was subject to competing demands from each departmental head.

The first leadership task was to take control and stabilise the crisis. The plant was spread over a 30-acre site and the senior team rarely met. On his first day, John called together the senior team and explained why he was there. He also established two rules:

1. The senior team would meet on a daily basis – on Train 18! This would force them to deal with problems as they arose and to co-operate in finding solutions on a timely basis.

2. In a move analogous to "seizing the cheque book", he decreed that once a design had been signed off, no further design work was permitted without his explicit approval and that he would only consider further changes if they enhanced safety and/or reduced costs.

John also asked each key manager, for review the following day, to produce a list of issues that were preventing their teams from delivering on time and on spec. Having got all the problems on the table, the managers were forced to co-operate to resolve them at their daily meeting – on Train 18. Train 18 was delivered on time and without defects or complaints and the immediate crisis was averted.

The next leadership task was to address the underlying processes that had given rise to the crisis and prevent a recurrence. John started with the organisational structure. The matrix organisation was dismantled. Projects were at the heart of the business and this was reflected in a project-driven structure, with the Project Director given both responsibility and accountability for delivery. Project offices were built at the centre of the site and regular team meetings were held there once Train 18 had been delivered. John visibly led from the front, taking personal responsibility for the first project (Train 18) and walking the two half-mile-long assembly lines twice daily, to stay close to the production process and address problems as and when they arose.

Despite "freezing" the design process and getting Train 18 out on time and to spec, the trains coming off the lines were still hugely over budget, driven by inefficiencies in production and assembly. In particular, there was an inability to complete allocated work within the required stage of assembly. Consequently, the problems rolled forward to the next stage and by the end of the line there were numerous incomplete sections and a huge snagging list to address.

John did not have extensive production experience, but he knew that the company needed a better way to operate and that "seeing was believing". He identified leading edge companies operating in similar fields and selected one – Jaguar – as an example of what could be achieved. Jaguar's management allowed John to take coach loads of workers to visit their plants and learn from their experience. This allowed him to build a shared vision of a better way of operating. Over the next few months, several process changes were implemented and unit rate costs dropped towards budgeted levels. However, step changes were needed in the technical process and this required expertise beyond the existing management's capability. John drew on the deep engineering expertise available in the wider parent company group, using French engineers to challenge current work practices and re-engineer the production line. In order to implement change, he would shut down a production line for a day or even for two weeks in one instance. This had never been done before but it sent a powerful message to the workforce: "We are not going on until it's fixed." By the end of John's tenure, the company was delivering 2.5 trains per week, a remarkable turnaround in performance that allowed him to negotiate away any threat of liquidated damages from the customer.

Probably more important than a few decisive symbolic moves is the way in which the turnaround leader often has to instil discipline into an organisation's processes. Empowerment, and the accompanying delegation that goes with it, may be important ingredients in building

an appropriate organisation for the future, but are often inappropriate for short-term process improvements. For example, in turning
around a shipyard that had a large Ministry of Defence contract, the
turnaround executive knew that the only way the contract could be
profitable was to ensure that all extra work, no matter how small, was
recorded. He also required top quality work (*"if I can't eat my break-
fast off the deck of this boat when it sails, this yard shuts"*). To ensure
that this happened he would arrive at any time of the day or night
and check the detail. Such visible hands-on leadership, focusing on
the detail, is often necessary in a turnaround. At Stolt Offshore, Tom
Ehret adopted a similar hands-on approach to ensure that rigorous
standards were established for bidding, contracting and risk assessment (see Box 8.4).

---

**Box 8.4    Stolt Offshore**

Stolt Offshore SA ("SOSA") is one of the world's leading contractors to the offshore oil and gas industry, building and in-
stalling pipelines and other structures to bring oil and gas from
the seabed to the surface in deep-water locations around the
world. Formerly a subsidiary of the Stolt-Nielsen Group, a
Norwegian conglomerate, SOSA sailed into troubled waters in
2002/2003 after an acquisition spree in the late 1990s.

Until 1997, SOSA was a profitable North Sea operator. A global
expansion strategy was executed through a series of over-priced
and poorly integrated acquisitions. In particular a "turn key"
contractor called EPTM was acquired in France but was subject
to little control or oversight from the acquirer. EPTM entered
into a number of substantial fixed price contracts for construction work offshore West Africa on poorly negotiated terms, in
a bid to buy market share. By the end of 2002, it was apparent that substantial losses would be incurred on these contracts
and debt levels soared as contractual disputes arose and SOSA
funded the losses.

In Spring 2003, a new leader – industry veteran Tom Ehret –
was appointed as CEO, with a mandate to restore the business
to the levels of profitability enjoyed by its peers. Tom's immediate task, assisted by new CFO Stuart Jackson, was to stabilise

the crisis. While work commenced on addressing the financial challenges faced by the company (see Box 10.3), Tom took operational control. He immediately put a halt to all tendering activity while he implemented rigorous risk management and review procedures, to ensure that further loss-making contracts were not being accepted. For the first few months every tender, whether for $1 million or $100 million, required Tom's approval. He also dismantled the matrix management structure that had made responsibility for the catastrophic projects opaque at best. He established a clear structure of regional managing directors, each responsible and accountable for all projects and the P&L within his region.

It took several months to get to the bottom of the problems on the "legacy" EPTM contracts. By the time this had been achieved, the necessary provisions made and the acquired assets written down to market value, 80% of the company's net worth had been eliminated. It was critical to get to the truth, and when project managers were found to be holding back information or concealing problems, they were fired, thus sending a message to the workforce that such behaviour would not be tolerated.

In parallel, Tom developed a strategy for recovery: the "Blueprint" that he communicated throughout the organisation in a series of roadshows and to external stakeholders, in particular the lenders. The strategy focused the business on three areas where SOSA had a distinct competitive advantage and required an exit from all non-core assets or activities. It was supported by a framework of new commercial disciplines, which would be set and enforced by a new corporate team of functional heads, working alongside the regional managing directors. Seventy per cent of the senior management team were changed over the course of a few months to ensure that the capabilities and attitudes were in place to make this happen. In particular, Tom instilled group-wide engineering standards and project management disciplines, including monthly reviews of every contract. Most importantly, rigorous standards were established for bidding, contracting and risk assessment. Tenders that were not presented for review in the correct format, or did not meet the new risk management criteria, were not submitted to customers, regardless of the impact on the order book. Tom was determined to embed the new disciplines and was prepared to turn away business in the short term in order to achieve this.

Tom had to rely heavily on his track record and reputation after nearly 30 years in the industry to retain the support of key customers and suppliers and spent much of his time in direct communication with them. His personal credibility was critical to SOSA continuing to win work during a period of tremendous uncertainty and instability. In addition, he had a very clear vision of what needed to be done and with the support of his new management team, quickly brought the "Blueprint" to life. Within 12 months, SOSA had generated over $100 million from the sale of non-core assets, collected over $100 million of disputed contractual payments from customers, won the largest contract in its history while rigorously applying the new commercial disciplines and substantially reduced its cost base, demonstrating its viability and paving the way for a full-scale financial restructuring.

The leadership role in achieving critical process improvements is often underestimated and, as a result, processes get only a "quick fix" and do not provide the foundation for sustainable recovery. The leader has a fine balancing act to maintain. He or she must combine hands-off management to allow ownership and people development while, at the same time, being involved in the detail.

At Lee Cooper, for example (see Chapter 7, Box 7.3), the main process improvements were in the supply chain and in the Tunisian factory. In the factory £1m was saved in the first 12 months and an additional £0.5 million in year 2 (20% of operational costs in total), while lead times were reduced from 26 weeks to 8 weeks. How was this achieved? According to Paul Hick:

*"We set the Tunisian factory management the challenge of becoming a world-class manufacturing unit with our full support. They set up 8 project teams of middle managers delivering 18 projects, each sponsored by a member of the executive – their enthusiasm and motivation at delivering these results was infectious between the teams and*

*inspirational to watch"... For the international group as a whole we brought together the 65 senior and middle managers for an annual two-day workshop for three years. In the first, the proportion of time spent presenting by the executive was 80% of the time. This was their pride and achievement in delivering their plan (rather than the executives). The year on year visible transformation in marketing, market development, product innovation, retail development, supply chain improvement and manufacturing was powerful and motivational for the whole team."*

# Using Advisers as Leaders

We are not great advocates of using consultants and advisers in turnaround situations, since by definition they are not decision makers and implementers. However advisers can sometimes play a crucial leadership role in bringing about change, if they can have the support of a chief executive who is prepared to "do what they say". To be effective, advisers have to have personal credibility and the energy and passion to push management into decision making and action. Most management consultants are not suitable for turnaround situations since they lack the practical experience of getting action quickly. Change management has become a fashionable term but most of those who practise it in consultancy firms either lack credibility with top teams or take a cumbersome approach – which is too slow (and often too expensive), at least in the early stages of a turnaround.

Box 8.5 shows an example of an approach where the adviser played a real leadership role in achieving dramatic change in some critical processes over a 10-week period. If this facilitation style of leadership is to work, the CEO has to accept and support the adviser. Usually by the time a company is in trouble the CEO has retrenched mentally and is not open to outsiders doing what he blatantly ought to be doing himself. In the example in Box 8.5 the CEO was under a lot of pressure and was only too pleased to have the new finance director take the initiative of bringing in an outside adviser as a facilitator. While the company made rapid progress as the result of this outside intervention, it was not a surprise to anyone when the CEO was eventually replaced several months later!

**Box 8.5    Example of how Advisers can Lead Critical Process Change in a Turnaround**

The UK division of a multinational consumer goods company with UK sales of over £600 million was still profitable but seriously under-performing. One of the big strategy consultancy focus had developed a new strategy for the business two years earlier and there were four separate firms of change management consultants working on different initiatives. None of this activity, however, was producing bottom line results. A new finance director was the trigger for bringing in an external turnaround adviser with a brief to focus on the demand generation side of the business. While the cost base of the business was an issue, the plants supplying the UK were not under the control of the UK division.

*Approach*

The adviser took the following seven-step approach:

- Reviewed the existing strategic plan and current market data.

- Facilitated an initial two-day Board workshop to challenge the relevance of each core element of strategy, to review progress to date and to identify the current strategic priorities.

- At the same time he undertook a rigorous analytical review of the key assumptions driving the financial performance of the business in the light of customer and competitor conditions. He did this by "drilling down" into each key component of the budget and doing a reality check against recent historical data.

- He facilitated a further Board workshop at which the strategy was modified, and it was agreed to focus on five areas crucial to the delivery of the new strategy over the next 12 months.

- Five project teams, each led by a director, were assembled to prepare action plans for each of the key areas, and these were facilitated by the adviser.

- The results of the project teams were reviewed and agreed at two further one-day Board workshops facilitated by the adviser.

- The adviser project managed and monitored the implementation of the action plans.

*Results*

The project achieved the following results:

- A fundamental shift in marketing strategy and tactics to focus resources into the areas with the most potential for strategic advantage over competitors.

- The new product development process and associated organisational support was improved to reduce new product lead time by 50%.

- The customer base was regrouped into more relevant sectors and the sales approach was aligned to each one.

- Unnecessary and inappropriate activities that wasted already scarce resources were identified and eliminated.

- Revenue and margin growth was achieved within six months of starting the process.

# 9

# Leading Organisational Change

FOR A COMPANY TO GO THROUGH A TURNAROUND AND reach a stage of sustainable recovery usually requires fundamental change to the internal processes (see previous chapter) and the organisational culture. However, as they have neither the time nor patience, the financial stakeholders in a turnaround are often not prepared to wait and support deep-seated organisational change. As soon as the business is stabilised and/or shows improved profitability, they may want to sell their investment. In most other cases, the turnaround leader wants to leave after stabilisation is complete but before a sustainable recovery is guaranteed. There is therefore a limit to the organisational change that can be achieved when the turnaround leader either moves on after six months or has a reward package geared only to short-term results. These individuals leave it to subsequent management to rebuild the organisation and bring about a fundamental change in culture.

The organisational change process actually begins as soon as the turnaround leader starts to show leadership – usually by communicating to the organisation why he or she has arrived (see Chapter 4). The normal psychological reaction of most managers and employees when faced with this situation is to feel threatened, in which case they may "close down" and be resistant to change.

In the very early stages of the turnaround, there may be very little sign of change for most managers and employees because the turnaround leader is likely to be heavily involved in implementing emergency measures to generate cash and holding frequent discussions with key stakeholder groups. However, as soon as his or her attention is turned to changing the management team, introducing new tight control systems, cost reduction and other critical activities necessary to stabilise the company, more and more people will start to feel the pressure for change. Key managers will recognise that unless they accept the need for change and implement change rapidly, they will be removed. Financial and management controls will emphasise targets and accountability. Early cost reduction measures will result in some people working harder, under-performing colleagues being fired and a recognition that jobs are not secure. Morale may decline as the changes start to bite. If all of this is supported by well-planned and frequent communication, as is usually the case with experienced turnaround leaders, the organisation culture will start to change – but slowly.

> *"When a company has been poorly managed for a long time managers and staff alike will probably be quite cynical about senior management. They will have seen top management saying one thing and doing another, hiding the truth, not communicating and failing to deliver as promised. Turnaround leaders are used to this and know that if they are to develop a more performance-oriented culture they must engage staff in the change process. They must explain decisions and demonstrate that they are being objective and fair."*

However communications alone are not enough. Before people change their behaviour in a lasting way something more than good communication is necessary. It is necessary to involve people who are willing to change in building the new organisation. Unfortunately, in the early stages of a turnaround where survival is the only objective, the turnaround leader and his or her management team do not have the time to involve large numbers of people either in decision making itself or in discussing the appropriate implementation processes. They tend to adopt an autocratic approach to get the short-term results (as discussed in Chapters 4 and 5) that are required, but in so doing they have not really changed how people think and work.

The most important organisational lever for short-term change is, of course, changing the senior management. The more that are changed the bigger the opportunity for kick-starting the development of a new culture. The credibility of a new management team can provide a strong base for rebuilding morale as the turnaround gains momentum. The removal of the previous management releases energy. The other short-term levers that can drive short-term performance improvement are:

- Simplifying and clarifying the organisation structure.

- Building ownership and commitment to change by involving staff in the improvement process.

- Ensure accountability through the introduction of simple performance measurement systems.

- Continuing to "over-communicate".

- Aligning rewards and incentive compensation to the turnaround goals.

- Training in focused areas to support critical process improvements.

In all these areas nothing will happen without the drive and commitment of the turnaround leader. Developing new incentive schemes and identifying emergency training needs are clearly managerial tasks but, as with everything else in a turnaround, the leader needs to be involved in overseeing the details and project manage the processes if the desired results are to be achieved.

## Simplifying The Organisation Structure

We explained in our earlier book, *Corporate Turnaround*, why changes to the organisation structure should be kept to a minimum in the first stages of a turnaround to avoid the risks always associated with structural change. While the general opinion of turnaround leaders is that changing the organisation structure should be avoided if possible, particularly before stabilisation is complete, it can nevertheless be a useful tool for simplifying the business and gaining direct control over key parts of the company. In the longer term, as the leader begins to delegate and empower, more decentralisation can be appropriate and the organisation structure can be adapted accordingly.

However, we did identify several situations where structural change can be a key ingredient of the turnaround process. One of these was to help to gain management control over the business. This happened at Marconi, where Mike Parton collapsed the corporate head office and the three operating divisions into one structure. Not only did this take costs out by reducing the senior management team from 52 to 12 (excluding the effect of disposals) and do away with fiefdoms, but also centralised control over the 12 operating units that remained after the divestment programme.

Many companies in distress have confused and complicated organisation structures, which have often been a contributing factor to the organisation's troubles. The most important organisational change a new leader can often make is to simplify the organisation structure. In the process, roles and responsibilities can be clarified and accountability improved. This is particularly true in large companies with multiple business units in different geographies and/or different sectors. As one chief executive said to us:

> "The company got into trouble in the first place because the business unit general managers were always able to point the finger at other units or functions when they missed their budgets . . . it was a complete blame culture with no real accountability . . . you cannot talk about synergy and leveraging capabilities in a turnaround . . . you must simplify the structure and focus managers on their own businesses."

## Building Commitment To Change

We see the biggest variation in leadership styles when we analyse how turnaround leaders manage organisational change. Some do not even attempt it – they are the short-term "transactional" leaders for whom people management skills are not an organisational priority when survival is the issue and, for them, motivational aspects of leadership are seen as a luxury. A few are transformational leaders building for the longer term. Most turnaround leaders, however, are somewhere in between the two ends of this spectrum. The difference lies in their personal style and philosophy based on a combination of personality attributes and prior experience. Sometimes the demands of the business require an immediate culture change (see Box 9.1).

---

### Box 9.1    Organisational Change Critical to Turnaround

Bill Price was brought in to turn around a family controlled office-moving company, where the bank was worried about its £5 million overdraft which was poorly secured. Management was a shambles, priorities were unclear; and there were a lot of serious quality issues and customer complaints. Bill described it as follows:

*"There were six females and four male dancers and a choreographer working in the company! There was nobody responsible for quality control. So together with the bank we forced out the owners, fired the dancers and brought in a real 'sergeant major' from one of the competitors as quality control manager. We had to coach him not just to bludgeon people all the time but also to have a softer side, rewarding staff with a £50 bonus for quality improvements. We completely turned around customer satisfaction levels but it required a huge culture change. . . . Sometimes the medium term issues need to be done."*

---

An increasing number of turnaround leaders now recognise that if they are to fix the business they must start to involve the middle management levels and below in the change process soon after arrival. The autocratic approach, while effective in the short term to ensure survival, will not provide the foundations necessary to fix the business. Even turnaround executives who stay only a short period (e.g. less than six months) and focus on short-term wins say it is important to push decisions down:

*"Pushing decisions down to incumbent management starts to breed a sense of self-reliance within the organisation."*

This practitioner's approach is to try to persuade the organisation to be more decisive by making people take responsibility if they want to achieve the outcome they prefer:

*"It is important people learn not to be afraid to make decisions which means they must be allowed to make the occasional mistake . . . . . Management gets in the way of people trying to do a job. People actually want to do a job well."*

Giving people freedom to do their job and achieve goals can be difficult if the leadership style of the previous management was autocratic
and hierarchical. In such situations it takes much longer to loosen
things up and get people to come forward and take responsibility.

Unlike the insolvency practitioner who can rely on the power inherent
in his or her legal position, the turnaround leader has to rely on his or
her ability to get people on board. One turnaround practitioner tries
to *"empower all the managers and employees so they collectively make the
decision on who the non-performers are and who should be asked to leave"*.
He goes on to say:

> *"I believe in listening to employees and allowing them to make the right
> decision for the company. My style is not about taking full control of
> everything and directing . . . believe in empowering people and making
> them see the desired goal. A single person cannot make the complete
> turnaround . . . until ownership is transferred to all employees it is
> difficult to achieve a true turnaround."*

This practitioner's leadership style has been heavily influenced by the
state of some businesses he has taken over which had previously been
through "a so-called turnaround". These businesses had been poorly
run by turnaround managers who had a "frantic autocratic style" –
everything had to be done today – and where they did not **listen** to
what incumbent managers and employees had to say.

Other practitioners emphasise how it is important early on in the process to share understanding and decision-making. One practitioner
generates early buy-in by organising what he calls strategy workshops
as a means of crystallising problems and identifying a recovery plan.
He acts as the workshop facilitator and finds that the process generates a strong sense of buy-in (not very dissimilar from the adviser's
approach outlined in box 8.5).

Involving people early on would appear to be beneficial since, in most
turnarounds, the answers are sitting there within the organisation.
However, virtually all the practitioners emphasise the need to maintain tight controls until the company has been stabilised. In practice
what we see is a gradual relaxation of the initial very tight controls
as the most urgent problems are solved and a recovery plan has been

put in place. One practitioner says that she explains face-to-face with the management how she intends to work with them:

> *"I let them know I will be specific, insultingly so, and closely monitoring them in the first assignment. I will then be less so with the following tasks as mutual trust starts to build."*

Close monitoring of activities means just what it says. In the initial stages, turnaround leaders will have progress meetings at least daily and sometimes more frequently, to ensure that results are achieved. One turnaround practitioner we know has a meeting at the beginning of the day and at the end – and no one goes home until the day's tasks are completed! Others talk about producing and monitoring action plans but "nothing is ever more than 10 days away". The process is very hands-on and controlled directly by the turnaround leader or one of his or her trusted "side kicks".

Early involvement does mean some delegation and the start of empowerment, but it is a long way from the classic textbook definition of empowerment. You cannot empower an organisation that lacks discipline and processes, otherwise chaos will ensue. Empowerment in a turnaround means *involvement* not *delegation*, and only slowly is this released as the organisation moves into transformation mode. The leadership style is likely to remain highly centralised and tightly controlled until performance is assured:

> *"I give managers the flexibility to innovate and improve around the new strategy. . . . But any nasty surprise will most likely result in the termination of the relevant manager's employment."*

Contrary to popular belief many turnaround leaders, particularly those who are there beyond the crisis stabilisation stage, go out of their way to try to convince people to change. Paul Hick, for example, at Lee Cooper (see Box 7.3) retained people who were slow and resistant to change but those who were "obstacles" were asked to leave. This view is echoed by another practitioner who says:

> *"I prefer to understand the nature of resistance and deal with it by explaining my objectives and trying to understand the reason for resistance. If I am unable to convince the individual and build a cooperative process, I will terminate his or her employment."*

It is obvious from talking to practitioners that they are clear on where they are going and what they are trying to achieve. They may be flexible on how it is done but will not let anyone stand in the way of achieving it. This is best summed up in the following quote:

> *"I try to involve as many people as possible in formulating a problem and finding the solution. On the surface it looks like a collective decision-making process but in reality . . . I arrive with a clear decision in my mind. If this decision does not find support among my colleagues, I assume responsibility and insist on the decision I believe is the best one."*

Involving lots of people is what Patrick O'Sullivan did at Zurich Financial Services in the UK where he used the GE Work Out method to involve all levels of his organisation in looking for improvements. However, he was equally tough with under-performers in the management team (see Box 9.2).

---

**Box 9.2   Culture Change at Zurich Financial Services (UK)**

When Patrick O'Sullivan was appointed chief executive of Eagle Star insurance in 1997, he had no idea how bad the financial situation was. Three months later it was announced that Eagle Star was to be acquired by Zurich Financial Services, and would be merged with their UK general insurance business. Patrick became Chief Executive of the combined entity when the merger was concluded. Right from the start he attempted to involve all employees in generating quick wins. With a background in GE Capital, O'Sullivan used the GE Work Out Process to help him. The process* allowed employees to submit initiatives to the management team at town hall style meetings. The only rules were:

- The initiatives had to come from the employees, usually those on the front line.

- They had to be capable of implementation in 6–12 weeks.

* See Dave Ulrich, Steve Kerr and Ron Ashkenas, The GE Work-Out, McGraw-Hill, 2002.

---

- Management had to take an immediate decision as to whether to implement the initiative or reject it. The only acceptable answers were "yes" or "no". No further review or analysis was permitted.

- The employees' line managers could not over-rule the decision or obstruct the implementation in any way.

This process was a powerful tool, both to build employee morale and involvement in the turnaround and to generate multiple ideas for improvement customer services, reducing costs or operating cash.

However, the challenge was to get the idea of constant change embedded and make it happen on an ongoing basis. He says:

*"How many companies go through rapid change and then go backwards because they have not learned to make change a permanent part of what they do?"*

He acknowledges that it was very difficult and required total commitment and dedication, but as he says:

*"You must get buy-in so that people feel ownership of the new environment and want to work together."*

Deep-seated change necessitated tough people decisions:

*"If the culture was to change fundamentally I had to change front to back . . . not just get rid of the senior management team (which he did) but all the permafrost and the only way to find them is to get in the front line yourself."*

As an example, he relates how he observed a senior executive continuing to exhibit behaviour inconsistent with the values he was trying to embed. He gave him a chance but on the third occasion he took him out of a meeting and dismissed him on the spot:

*"I couldn't afford for the team to see X was bucking the trend of what we wanted to happen."*

O'Sullivan believes that the workout process was fundamental in helping to achieve sustainable culture change. He says:

*"There is no simple way of doing it but we had to go fast, deep and take dramatic action to make things change."*

## Accountability and Performance Management

Making managers and employees accountable for meeting budgets, targets, deadlines, etc., is one of the critical levers of short-term organisational change. It is the first step in building a performance or results-oriented culture. In most turnaround situations we find that managers have not been held accountable for results, and the existence of a performance management system is no guarantee that managers are accountable. It is only when senior management are seen to deal with poor performance by removing individuals from their jobs that the concept of accountability starts to have traction. Even then, if the reasons for removal are not clearly communicated within the organisation (perhaps through the management "grapevine"), change will be very slow.

In the early days of a turnaround, the notion of accountability can instil fear into many employees if it is not seen to be "fair". There may be some short-term wins by continually communicating the need for accountability and firing some under-performers, but true accountability requires a simple performance management system to support it. Most performance management systems are overly complicated and designed by under-employed HR departments. What is required is something simple, objective and aligned to the immediate needs of the business.

Interestingly, one of the mistakes Lou Gerstner made at IBM was his failure to put in such a system soon after arriving. It was only 18 months later, after a conversation with a senior colleague, that he realised he needed to turn his "win, execute, team" mantra into a simplified performance management system. The new Personal Business Commitment programme required managers to list their actions under the three headings – and this was linked to a new performance-indexed compensation system.

Performance management and rewards are closely linked in the minds of most turnaround leaders (even though HR professionals often like to keep them separate from a personal development perspective). Changing reward systems – particularly bonus and incentive systems – is a key component in many turnaround strategies. The leadership skills of the turnaround practitioners are clearly important in the way they communicate why reward systems are being changed, and ensuring that they are seen to be fair.

Strong turnaround leaders are sometimes able to negotiate very attractive incentive packages for themselves and their top management teams. At Marconi, for example, Mike Parton and his team obtained 9% of the equity after financial restructuring.

## Communications

Every turnaround leader interviewed for the research underlying this book stressed the importance of communications during the turnaround process. It underpins every successful turnaround. Ongoing communication with managers and employees is absolutely essential:

> *"Unless people tell you you are sounding 'like an old record' you are not getting your message through."*

Many companies in trouble have historically had a hierarchical structure with poor communications, and when a new leader arrives with a more informal style and an open-door policy there is perceived to be an immediate change. In the early days of a turnaround the biggest problem for the turnaround leader is likely to be the inability and often unwillingness of senior and middle management to communicate the new leader's message down the organisation. Not surprisingly, many turnaround leaders feel they need to bypass the existing management communications system (if indeed one exists) and talk directly to all employees. In large, geographically dispersed businesses this is not always easy and video conferencing, conference calls, e-mails and other technology may be employed to assist the communication process. After stabilisation has been achieved and the leader turns his or her attention to fixing the business, the best leaders will ensure that an effective communication cascade is in place and will discipline senior and middle managers who do not comply.

The leader needs to establish a regular process that must balance the need for frequency with having content worthy of communicating. Weekly communication is usually about right. Communication must have some impact and be interesting to ensure that people remain focused. People like public praise: it is important to use communication to reward and motivate.

Communication is, as we know, a two-way process and the sooner the turnaround leader engages in dialogue with the staff the sooner he or she can begin to have a real impact on organisational behaviour. The informal style of most turnaround leaders means that they chat freely and they practise "management by walking around", asking questions and seeking opinions. As the crisis of survival subsides, the communication programme may become more institutionalised, but the leader should be careful not to resume "business as normal" too soon. One successful leader developed a three-pronged communication programme as follows:

- Talking with the CEO – monthly meetings with groups of employees.

- Management workshops between employees and supervisors.

- An annual workforce assembly (on a plant by plant basis) where the CEO shared results and plans with the workforce.

In earlier research, one of the authors identified improved communication as the most noticeable aspect of organisational change during a typical turnaround. This is echoed by one turnaround executive who says:

> *"My prime organisational concern is that the openness and communication that I foster remains after my departure."*

## Transition to Transformation

To achieve long-lasting sustainable recovery – which we believe is only possible for a relatively small percentage of all the companies that get into trouble (say 20% at the most) – the turnaround leader has to exit or change his or her leadership style. A few are demonstrably able to do this and are motivated to do so – usually by equity ownership. Their secret is their ability not just to involve people but to delegate real responsibility as far down the organisation as possible. Only then is a real and lasting change of culture brought about.

Those leaders who go beyond turnaround into transformation start to involve their people as early as they can, although, initially, they are always directive and if necessary autocratic. They are, however, aware of the need for culture change. Thus at Riva Plc, a software company where Peter Giles is chairman, he personally developed and facilitated workshops with teams from different countries in order to rethink products and processes. He believes that teamwork was an important foundation stone to achieve behaviour change and hence culture change in the organisation. Although the consultative process was very hard and painful in the beginning, participation and interaction clearly helped employees to implement change more effectively.

Successful transition to sustainable recovery requires wide delegation and empowerment. Until "ownership" is transferred to a wide body of employees sustainable recovery cannot be achieved. This is true leadership, and is well illustrated by the transformation at Zurich Financial Services (UK) – see Box 9.2

For delegation and empowerment to be successful, however, the turnaround leader has to be "hands-on" in making it happen. John Ball at Libertys department store believes that the key to change is for him not to take on any of the decision-making. However, he attends all staff meetings to ensure that employees are empowered to develop their ideas:

> *"If an issue is raised at a meeting I push the issue back to the staff and ask them to come up with a solution. I force the staff to set and control the agenda and priorities for their own areas. By doing this I push ownership and responsibility back to the staff who can do something about the issue. I am only interested in ensuring that the decisions fit into the overall recovery plan."*

As the company moves out of turnaround, the steely determination of the company doctor remains. He continues to have clear goals and believes in what he is trying to achieve. Thus at software company Riva, Peter Giles has no hesitation in firing people if they are unwilling to share their knowledge or are too bureaucratic in their approach. He knows the type of culture he is trying to build for the long term and will not be pushed off course.

One of the best examples of where a leader radically changed his leadership style was shown at the Clares Group (see Box 9.3). As the organisation progressed out of crisis and a new strategy was put in place, John Ensall, the CEO, increasingly relaxed control. He set levels for capital expenditure, employment, pay reviews and stock purchasing but gave the five divisional directors progressively more leeway to run their business units. Over the next 18 months as the directors continued to meet their business plan objectives, they were given more and more flexibility and power. During this time John changed from an autocratic leadership style to a much more collaborative style, where he saw himself as *"more of a facilitator, encourager, supporter and counsellor than a chief executive"*. This is well summed up in a quotation from one of his employees:

> *"When he (John) first came into the business we were very scared of him.... (We) thought he was a dictator who thought he was God's gift. However we appreciated that he had knowledge and intellect... he knew what he wanted to do. Now we see him as a colleague, a good friend, a CEO who gives us power and real responsibility but who is very supportive and able to discuss things with us."*

---

### Box 9.3    The Growth Phase At Clares Group

*(See also Box 7.5)*

The turnaround process at Clares Group lasted for almost two years. By the end of Year 3, sales had doubled as a result of organic growth and acquisition and return on capital employed was over 40%.

During the growth phase of the organisation, John's leadership style changed dramatically. While he continued to have very close relationships and a lot of communication with his directors, the relationship was different from that during the early days of the turnaround. John began to play more of a consultancy role, acting more like a coach than a direct manager of his five directors. The managers saw him as someone who was involved with the overall direction of the company rather than with the day-to-day operations. Managers seemed to appreciate their power and preferred to be left to do their daily work.

Contrary to his early days in the business, John rarely met with his staff and employees in a formal way, leaving this responsibility with the five directors. Instead, John walked around the organisation in a very informal, even social manner, "chatting" to his employees as he passed by. Communication from John also changed considerably. Since John was less involved with the company's processes, he rarely held one-sided lecture-type meetings or posted memos on SEC's notice-boards. Instead John spent his time on Clares long-term strategy, acquisitions and shareholder communications.

---

An example of a dramatic transformation in a relatively short period of time is provided by the South African diamond mining company Trans Hex, to which we have already referred in earlier chapters. Calvyn Gardner involved all the workforce in the change process that led to a significant culture change – and although this was so important it is often difficult to achieve in a geographically dispersed organisation (see Box 9.4).

---

**Box 9.4    Culture Change At Trans Hex**

*(See also Boxes 4.2 and 6.2)*

By the time Calvyn Gardner left Trans Hex in March 2004, the company had not only been turned around financially but had embarked on an ambitious growth strategy involving new mine investments in Angola ("world class assets – better by miles than the rest of our mines") and investment in off-shore mining. However, his lasting achievement is the culture change he instilled into the organisation. There is now a clear emphasis on teamwork, mutual respect and racial tolerance. This is most noticeable at the mines where a combination of a changed leadership style and Gardner's actions in promoting employee welfare have contributed to almost a family atmosphere. Gardner believes that the family atmosphere makes possible the corporate discipline he requires: *"Everyone here believes in what we are trying to do. There is the belief that if you pull your weight and you work hard, you will grow with this company."* Corporate discipline dictates that individual performance is measured on a "per head" productivity basis. But at the same time, employees are encouraged to grow and improve their *communal* as well as *individual* opportunities through various training programmes offered by the company.

Gardner has involved all the workforce in the change process giving them opportunities to take the initiative and explore improvement possibilities as they identify them. Gardner describes his approach:

*"Some of the guys (at the mines) had some good ideas. Maybe they weren't 'perfect', but they were 'good'. And once you start letting guys put good ideas in, you're one step better than where you were before. That is truly the philosophy here. Never let the perfect be the enemy of the good. If it's better, even if it's just 1% better, do it. Okay? Just do it. Because what does it do? It builds confidence. The guy gets success. And next time, it's not going to be a 1% improvement he brings you, it's going to be 15%. But if you say no, don't do it, and it was a good idea, then the next*

*time, I'm afraid, you might not get your 15% improvement the*
*day you try to get it."*

This philosophy promotes a culture that works well with the
geographical and operational realities with which Gardner
must contend. He simply cannot be everywhere executing his
turnaround strategy. He has to be able to rely on his teams at
each mine to do that for him.

*"One must understand where we are: our mines are remote,*
*they're all over the country. And in different countries. We oper-*
*ate in Namibia in addition to South Africa. We're in Botswana,*
*and we're in Angola. So in my opinion, you have to get a core*
*team of people around you that actually believe in what you are*
*doing as much as you do. You have to know that these guys that*
*you are putting in these remote places will do the job as if you*
*were there yourself. If we were all in one building I can image*
*that might be a bit easier. But when you are in all these remote*
*areas – even on vessels at sea, operating 250 km off-shore – I*
*need to know that what we are trying to do is in fact being done*
*in those remote areas, where I may only see these guys once every*
*couple of months."*

Of necessity, Gardner has installed a culture at Trans Hex that
breeds its own continuing success.

Critical to changing the attitude of employees have been extensive communication exercises and tangible improvements to
employee welfare. Since taking the helm, Gardner has established a centralised health and safety department and improved
employee health and safety at all mines, with disabling injury
frequency down by over 50%. An AIDS awareness campaign
and employee assistance programme was introduced, and every
employee now receives training as regards racial tolerance and
black empowerment. Trans Hex is ahead of its peers in promoting black and coloured employee advancement within the
company – at every level – well beyond government established
quotas and ahead of government timetables set for achieving
more integrated firms.

# Exiting Gracefully

Knowing when to leave is a crucial leadership skill for the turnaround professional. Sometimes this is not the professional's decision as the investors may sell the company, or the exit parameters may be established in advance as part of the turnaround leader's contract. Where there is a choice, much will depend on the skills of the turnaround leader. As should be obvious from the previous chapters in this book, there is a spectrum of turnaround leaders from those who are essentially chief restructuring officers with a largely financial focus or have a short-term contract to lead the crisis stabilisation phase, to those who see themselves as the chief executives or chairmen who can lead a long-term transformation of the business.

Most turnaround practitioners have neither the interest nor the skills to run a business long term. They enjoy the hands-on style necessary in a crisis and are quickly bored when routine sets in. Many turnaround professionals are also aware that their skills are confined to the stabilisation phase. This is reflected in the following comments:

*"Most turnaround guys are bad long-term managers."*

*"I am not very good at the nurturing of ideas and bringing them to fruition. . . . My job is to ensure there is a self-sufficient management team in place by the end of the first year, at which point my role becomes advisory."*

*"My management style is not suited to ongoing management."*

It would seem that most turnaround leaders know when it is time to leave and do not overstay their welcome, as the following quotes illustrate :

*"You know when it's time to leave. The business or the situation stops changing dramatically, indicating that you are in a steady state."*

*"By the time it comes for you to leave you should really be irrelevant. The role is a bit strange; it's based on you working yourself out of a job. By the time I leave no one should notice the difference . . . that is*

*the perfect turnaround. You are not there to run the business for ever, you are there to provide some options for the stakeholders."*

*"The management team that is left behind should be capable of taking the organisation where I could not have."*

When the turnaround leader moves on, it is critically important that there is a solid foundation of good processes in place and that a new organisational culture has at least started "to take root". There are too many examples of where companies have slipped back to their old ways of operating as soon as the turnaround executive moves on. If this is the case, he or she has failed.

# 10

# Financial Restructuring

IT IS CLEAR THAT EVEN IF THE TURNAROUND LEADER CAN BLEND all the other key ingredients of a successful turnaround but the business is left unable to service its capital structure, all that effort will have been for nothing since covenant and other loan document breaches will soon recur. The financial structure of the company must invariably be renegotiated to align it to the needs and capacity of the new business that arises from implementation of the other key ingredients. A financial restructuring normally becomes necessary in companies where, consequential to many factors, the financial stakeholders' risk/reward balance has been distorted or broken. We say normally because in the case where investors acquire discounted debt with the intention of benefiting from an upcoming restructuring, they may actively precipitate a restructuring in order to maximize their returns.

The objectives of a financial restructuring are threefold:

1   To establish a stable capital structure, commensurate with the enterprise value and cash-generating capacity of the revitalised business

2   To ensure that the new capital structure reflects correctly the economic interests of those stakeholders who will support the company through its turnaround and does so on the basis of a balance that is satisfactory to themselves, other stakeholders and the company. The new structure will rarely be the same as existed at the time of the initial participation or investment, but will reflect the additional perceived and sometimes actual risk that exists in the relationship.

3   To restore the risk profile (particularly in relation to credit extended to the company) to that accepted at the time of making the

original credit available, subject to the requirements of the first two objectives. This is normally measured in terms of leverage and other financial ratios, asset coverage and other covenanted performance criteria.

In small and medium-sized companies, the capital structure is usually quite straightforward and depends on a key relationship with one or two domestic lenders. In such cases, the restructuring will often be negotiated directly between the company and its stakeholders, based on the business plan that has been developed as part of the turnaround process. The business plan shows the way to recovery and underlying financial models will indicate what the company can afford by way of debt service and amortisation. The restructuring process becomes considerably more complicated as companies grow and more financial stakeholders become involved in multi-level capital structures. In this chapter we have focused on the role of the restructuring leader in these more complex situations.

As in the other critical phases of the turnaround process, the turnaround or restructuring practitioner has to have the ability to "morph" between leadership and management during the financial restructuring process. He or she has to be both a detailed project manager, able to navigate through the fine print of detailed legal and commercial negotiations, and a visionary leader who can clearly articulate a financially viable "desired end state" that preserves greater value for stakeholders than the alternative of insolvency.

The leader's task is both to establish an end game for the process as well as aligning the multiple parties involved, to achieve a successful outcome to the negotiations. Within the firmament of broken promises, lack of initial understanding, and corporate and personal agendas typical of most turnaround situations, even a modest restructuring can quickly involve 50 to a 100 people. If the leader is to be successful, he or she has to bring order, create calm, maintain focus and find a way forward that offends the least number of parties. The law provides for remedies where parties fail to agree, but it is usually the case that the application of insolvency procedures further reduces the value of the enterprise. The alternative, liquidation value is the ultimate yardstick against which the value preserved through a consensual restructuring is measured.

# The Restructuring Leader

As discussed in Chapter 6, leading financial restructuring is increasingly becoming a specialist role within the overall turnaround process. Our research revealed that very few of the generalist turnaround practitioners or company doctors we interviewed were habitually involved in this stage of the restoration of a sick company. The engagement of a specialist restructuring practitioner to lead the financial restructuring process is a relatively new trend brought about by the evolution of the capital markets, the increased complexities of corporate financial structures and the appreciation of financial stakeholders that consensual restructuring preserves value and therefore insolvency measures should be the very last resort – not the first.

Prior to the late 1980s, most enterprises were funded through bilateral lending, often by a single lender, with a heavy domestic focus as the lender and the enterprise were usually from the same country. From the mid-1990s onwards, multi-banked, syndicated facilities provided from lenders and investors of many different domiciles became common, together with significant increases in publicly traded debt, both investment grade and high-yield or "junk" bonds, and privately placed mezzanine debt and other instruments. For example, in a company (advised recently by one the authors) that has revenues approaching €200 million, the capital structure included funding from financial institutions in Italy, France, the UK and the USA. Bilateral and syndicated facilities were held in three tranches of senior and mezzanine debt plus subordinated shareholder loans. Such complexity is not uncommon today, fuelled in part by the rise in leveraged buy-outs and in part by the over-supply of liquidity, which has trickled down to smaller companies, enabling them to fund growth at a lower cost of capital.

In the early 1990s lenders operating in multi-bank situations or syndicates within the UK were subject to a voluntary protocol for distressed companies, policed by the Bank of England and known rather quaintly as "The London Approach". The Bank of England expected banks that held a licence to operate in the UK to "act like gentlemen" in supporting a company through its difficulties, regardless of their contractual rights as set out in the loan documentation. Inter-creditor disputes were settled behind closed doors with the influence of the Bank of England brought to bear when necessary. There was very little secondary debt trading and the same financial stakeholders were typically involved from the initial loan through to completion of a restructuring.

Today we have multiple creditor classes, financial stakeholders based in numerous jurisdictions, and extensive secondary debt trading across all classes of financial instruments. The newer entrants to the market were not familiar or enamoured of an approach that suggested they should not act in accordance with the rights enshrined in their loan documentation, and it did not take long for "The London Approach" to wither on the vine.

At the same time as capital structures have become more complicated, private equity has become a major influence in the capital markets. Today equity stakeholders more effectively resist the pressure of senior debtholders to 'give up and go away', leaving the enterprise value to be carved up among the creditors. In addition, a rescue culture has developed in the UK, with the leading commercial banks becoming increasingly reluctant to use insolvency legislation – preferring where possible to achieve a "consensual" restructuring without recourse to a formal insolvency process.

It is within this changed framework that we see the emergence of a new breed of restructuring leader – often referred to as the Chief Restructuring Officer or "CRO". There is a growing appreciation of the need for a central person or office to take overall responsibility for finding and implementing a restructuring solution acceptable to all parties.

> *"Time is short; strengthening management is always needed, but are the Board gutsy enough to make the appointment of a CRO team?"*

That, says Lachlan Edwards, European head of Restructuring at N.M. Rothschild & Sons, the investment bank, is the key management question.

The Chief Restructuring Officer (CRO) role originated in "Chapter 11" restructurings in the USA. Complex capital structures and the consequent requirement for specialist financial restructuring expertise have been a feature of the US market since the 1990s. As capital flows from the USA to Europe have increased, demand for similar expertise from both creditors and debtors has brought the CRO role to Europe.

The Chief Restructuring Officer works for the company, can be a special adviser to the chairman, the CEO or the Board and often joins the Board during the restructuring and turnaround process. He or she is often appointed at an early stage of the process at the insistence of the principal creditors, who may even make the appointment of a CRO a condition of support, for example, when a waiver of a breach of covenant is required. The CRO's objective is to assist the company to reach an agreement between all stakeholders on the future capital structure of the business. Box 10.1 provides a comprehensive description of the duties of a CRO.

---

**Box 10.1    The Role of the Chief Restructuring Officer**

- Manage the "working group" professionals who are assisting the company in the reorganisation process, or who are working for the company's various stakeholders, to improve co-ordination of their effort and individual work product to be consistent with the company's overall restructuring goals.

- Assist the company in implementing a rolling 13-week cash flow forecasting and monitoring process to provide on-time information related to the company's liquidity and assist the company with other treasury-related support as requested.

- Assist the company in the ongoing development of overall strategic and business plans, including analysing alternative strategic plans and exit strategies.

- Assist the company's management and its professionals specifically assigned to sourcing, negotiating and implementing any financing, in conjunction with the Plan of Reorganisation and the overall restructuring.

- Analyse performance improvement and cash-enhancement opportunities, including assisting with cost reduction

---

improvement initiatives, operational improvement initiatives, accounts receivable management and accounts payable process improvement opportunities.

- Assist the company and its professionals with the analysis and negotiation of the divestiture of any non-core assets or business lines in conjunction with considering other strategic alternatives.

- Assist management with assessing organisational and operational structure of the company and work with the company regarding potential changes and efficiencies.

- Oversee the communications and/or negotiations with outside constituents, stakeholders and their representatives.

- Review the company's information systems capabilities and make recommendations regarding cost savings and/or downsizing initiatives as requested.

In the remainder of this chapter we are going to focus on the role of the restructuring leader in the following critical activities:

- Achieving a standstill agreement
- Understanding stakeholders' agendas
- Understanding the corporate's needs
- Co-ordinating advisers
- Leading restructuring negotiations.

### Achieving a Standstill Agreement

Often a financial restructuring will commence with a "standstill agreement", which provides a stable platform from which the turnaround can be implemented. A standstill agreement is an agreement (not always legally binding) between the company and all its financial stakeholders whereby the financial stakeholders agree not to enforce their contractual rights against the company (for example, the right to demand repayment or enforce security over assets) subject to certain conditions. Stakeholders usually will not give up the rights to trade their interest during the standstill period; indeed, the company is likely to have to give up any rights it previously had to prevent such transfers of interest, as a condition of a standstill. The conditions to be complied with will normally include the company agreeing to:

- share specific information with its lenders on a regular basis;

- produce an achievable business plan by a given date which sets out details of the turnaround and how it will be implemented;

- the appointment of advisers with appropriate experience and competence to assist the company in meeting the conditions of the standstill;

- the appointment of advisers or reporting acountants (at the company's cost) to review the business plan and related information on behalf of the lenders;

- the creditors having certain additional rights in the event of a default of the standstill terms.

For a standstill to be achieved it is normally a prerequisite that the company has stabilised any immediate cash crisis and has sufficient funding available (based on a credible short-term cash flow forecast) to trade through the anticipated standstill period or has at least provided evidence that it has credible plans and actions in place to achieve this. It is also necessary to have established who the financial stakeholders are and have a good understanding as to their rights and exposures in the current circumstances. This was discussed in detail in Chapter 6, Stakeholder Management.

Many standstill agreements are entered into in the expectation that during the period of the standstill a viable plan will emerge. Obtaining this "breathing space" is extremely helpful to the turnaround process and is most commonly achieved where the company has agreed to engage experienced advisers and/or interim executives and the stakeholders have additional confidence in the process due to the credibility and experience of the individual or team. As discussed in Chapter 3, some practitioners may use the leverage afforded by their appointment to make a standstill or other explicit statement of stakeholder support a prerequisite to accepting an appointment. This may be feasible in bilateral relationships but is likely to be extremely difficult to achieve in a multi-creditor restructuring.

Achieving a standstill is not as straightforward as it may appear. As previously indicated, there is a well-established secondary market in stressed and distressed corporate debt and the creditors who made the original loans may no longer be involved when problems arise or may sell down their position during the course of restructuring negotiations, so the negotiating counter-party can change during the process. Different creditors will have different entry level exposure since those who have lent at par at the outset may well have sold down at a discount. These discounts are not disclosed (although trading prices are readily available) but the attitude of individual creditors to standstill requests will vary according to their actual exposure and their longer-term objectives; they may be unwilling to suspend any rights at all until a final restructuring has been achieved. As a consequence many restructurings take place without the benefit of a standstill agreement. These circumstances are particularly stressful for the company's management, who face the continuous threat of enforcement throughout the restructuring negotiations.

The negotiation of the standstill agreement is a critical stage in the rescue of the company since there will be no discussion about financial restructuring unless the creditors have formed an initial view that there is at least a chance of improving their position through a turnaround process. Creditors are being asked in a standstill to give up certain rights in exchange for the prospect of a better outcome; in order to do so, they have to be convinced that it is in their interest to do so and that the jam promised for tomorrow is worth significantly more than bread today. It is the role of the turnaround leader and/or specialist advisers that have been hired to help the company to persuade the creditors to sign up to the process, and this will depend as much on their personal credibility as on the terms on offer. As one senior banker said to us: *"It's not just a question of seeing numbers that show an improvement but that we have confidence in those who are going to implement the changes."*

Box 10.2 provides an example of a how AlixPartners negotiated a standstill agreement and subsequent restructuring agreement with the creditors of the JAL Group, a mid-sized corporate.

## Box 10.2    Financial Restructuring of JAL Group

JAL Group is the European market leader in safety shoe manufacturing and distribution, with annual revenues of €180 million on annual volumes of 11 million pairs of shoes and boots. Registered in Luxembourg, it has manufacturing plants in Tunisia and France and is headquartered in Italy.

|                        | €(millions) |
| ---------------------- | ----------- |
| Annual revenues        | 180         |
| Annual EBITDA (2003)   | 25          |
| Senior debt            | 119         |
| Mezzanine debt         | 43          |
| Shareholder loans      | 100         |
| Total employees        | 4000        |

In April 2004, AlixPartners met with the lead agents for the senior debt, following the transfer of the loan from the relationship team into the workout department. The company was in breach of covenants and the agent wished to introduce advisers to the company, with a view to helping the company through the difficulties it faced.

Soon after, AlixPartners met with the majority shareholder, a major private equity group based in Paris. Although the shareholders agreed with the banks' assessment that management and working capital control should be improved, they disagreed with the agent bank on other issues and wished to retain control of the situation.

AlixPartners was subsequently retained by JAL as its financial and turnaround adviser. The first steps involved establishing control, improving reliability of reported information and stabilising the financial position of the group. Meanwhile initiatives to improve operational performance were developed and implemented. It was clear that the group needed new capital and yet the stakeholders were not prepared to work together. For the sake of the company, the stakeholder dispute had to be brought to a head.

It was apparent to both major equity holders that they had no economic interest in the group, but with new investment that position might be restored. Whereas the private equity group held 56% of the equity as against the CEO's holding of 36%, these positions were reversed at the shareholders' loans level. These subordinated debts were held 35% by private equity and 65% by the CEO. The parties did not agree that the legal documentation reflected the commercial agreement between them and whereas one party wished to rely on the shareholders' agreement the other did not. AlixPartners needed to find a way through this unsatisfactory state of affairs in order to move forward.

With AlixPartners' support, the group achieved a standstill agreement with all its financial creditors for a period of four months, during which time the company agreed to produce an achievable business plan and develop a restructuring proposal that was acceptable to all the financial stakeholders. The business plan indicated that there was a good prospect of reversing the impairment in values for all classes of financial stakeholder over the next four years.

To obtain the standstill AlixPartners needed to obtain the support of all the warring stakeholders and convince them that while a resolution of their differences was critical, it would be of little value if the company failed in the meantime. For JAL Group to survive it needed a period of financial stability, and to achieve that it needed a standstill. A key condition of the standstill was that equity agreed to inject new money.

The equity holders were both asked to submit proposals of shareholder support to the company. The restructuring advisers were able to trade each party against the other for the company's benefit; however, it became obvious over time that the CEO's proposals were more favourable to the company. The process of selecting a supporting shareholder took far longer than timetabled and the standstill period was extended throughout 2004 by the lenders.

The process led to the development of a plan that incorporated the investment of new money by one of the equity stakeholders. Without the standstill the company would not have been able to continue to trade since it was continuously in breach of its covenants and other loan obligations.

In the end, these agreements were not completed, the senior and mezzanine stakeholders sold their debt into the secondary market and the group, with the help of AlixPartners, is now developing a solution with a new investor group. The equity stakeholders have exited as part of the new solution.

Box 10.3 describes how Rothschilds and AlixPartners deployed different skills to provide a breathing space for Royal Ahold while management focused on fixing the underlying operations.

### Box 10.3   Advisers' Role in Crisis Stabilisation at Royal Ahold

N.M. Rothschild ("Rothschilds") were the lead financial advisers to Royal Ahold, the third largest supermarket retailer in the world, whose balance sheet was ravaged following accounting irregularities and a possible fraud, mainly in its US operations. The key task was to stabilise the balance sheet and create a breathing space for management to implement a disposal programme and fix the operations.

At the start of February 2003, Ahold was an investment grade, blue chip company, based in Amsterdam but with more than 50% of its revenues and earnings in the USA. On 24 February 2003, Ahold made its key announcement about the irregularities. The consequence of this and other related events was a downgrade in the company's credit rating to sub-investment grade. As an immediate consequence of the rating decline, uncommitted bilateral lines fell away and facilities with ratings triggers were no longer available. The CEO and CFO both resigned, effective 10 March, and urgent refinancing was necessary to meet funding needs. In these situations not only is urgent advice and leadership required from investment bankers but management often needs strengthening to see it through the turbulent period. Companies in these circumstances also need

> different information and this can often prove difficult to obtain, analyse and understand
>
> Rothschilds worked quickly to repair the funding gap, negotiating with lenders an emergency liquidity facility of $2.75 billion on 3 March and a back-up securitisation facility. At the same time, AlixPartners provided interim management and advisory support to maximise cash generation from the operations. Crisis stabilisation on a major scale produced a breathing space and enabled a clean working capital opinion critical for a clean audit report.

## Understanding Stakeholders' Agendas

Whether or not a standstill is achieved, the first step in leading a financial restructuring is to know the parties, understand how they became involved, and determine whether and to what extent they wish to remain involved. The turnaround leader – be it the Chairman, Chief Executive or CRO – needs to have an in-depth understanding of the players in the process.

Financial stakeholders normally become involved in a company through a logical decision-making process in which they decide to make a commitment and advance credit for acceptable business returns. The atmosphere at that time is normally a positive since both parties have contributed to achieving their objectives by entering into a business relationship. From the financial stakeholders' point of view there will have been a financial assessment and the credit committee or other sanctioning body within the financial institution will have concluded that the risk–reward trade-off is acceptable.

A successful financial restructuring is helped if the leader develops a good understanding of how the parties first came together and what their expectations were at that time. Situations arise where a lead financial institution enters into an arrangement with a company but then syndicates its exposure or sub-participates with other financial institutions. This adds complexity and scope for misunderstanding and ill-will once the company hits troubled waters, since the syndicate members will tend to rely not only on the information memorandum provided at the time, but also on the representations and reputation of the syndicating institution and may have limited knowledge or understanding of the borrower. The restructuring leader will need to understand the position and expectations of these sub-participants and start to address the gaps in their knowledge as a precursor to any negotiations.

Over recent years the "going in position", which is how we describe the above, has become yet more complicated by the development of a secondary debt market. Now it is quite common, particularly in international financings, to find that the financial stakeholders are those who have acquired the interest of another, normally at a discount, at some time after the initial stakeholder became invested. This is particularly true for companies in financial distress. Indeed some stakeholders, such as so-called "hedge funds" or "vulture funds", will have acquired debt in a company with the sole purpose of acquiring a substantial equity interest on favourable terms through a subsequent restructuring, the so-called "loan-to-own" approach. Such stakeholders will have assessed the firm's potential based on information available in the market, as well as information received from the vendor financial stakeholder, who will have often only provided it on a "buyer beware" basis.

This "getting to know you" process will be repeated for each class of financial stakeholder, many of whom will have become involved at different price points, resulting in different agendas and objectives within the various classes as well as between classes of stakeholders. It is also very important to understand the financial institutions themselves: how they behave under stress and what may be acceptable to them as institutions as well as the style and agenda of the individuals who are negotiating on behalf of each institution.

Different financial institutions take different approaches. Less traditional creditors such as US bond holders or hedge funds are sometimes castigated by more traditional institutions for their approach to rescue situations, particularly as they take an increasingly active role in forcing corporate restructurings. However, others find their approach refreshingly clear since they are concerned with value and value alone and approach the restructuring process with the clear aim of leveraging whatever power they have to maximise value, for example, through exploiting opportunities or loopholes in contractual documentation, regardless of wider relationship or policy type biases. This contrasts with other, more traditional lenders who may be constrained by organisational policies or reputational considerations as to their position within the markets they serve. Stakeholders whose institutions rely on relationship banking are often concerned with the effects that an approach adopted in one restructuring may have on their business relationships elsewhere. This can lead to what can appear to be economically irrational behaviour in the particular circumstances.

The CRO or restructuring leader, who will normally be familiar with many if not all of the financial stakeholders, needs to clearly understand their corporate and personal positions in the particular circumstance. He or she needs to ensure that, in so far as is possible, the business plan and restructuring proposal addresses the issues and concerns of individual stakeholders and therefore is one that the stakeholders will be able to support. There are many points that are not materially significant to a company but are of value to particular stakeholders. The CRO needs to be aware of these and he or she needs to know when to "trade" them.

Some stakeholders may try to overplay their hand and the CRO needs to clearly understand the actual influence and power they have. He or she would do well to assume that the stakeholders will exercise their power to its utmost but also to understand the boundaries of their powers and keep all stakeholders within them. He or she needs to understand the relationship between institutions and can help broker deals, to enable the supportive creditors to remain in the process while others exit on acceptable terms. Inter-creditor arrangements may exist, that govern priorities and processes within a creditor class or between classes. Working closely with the company's legal advisers, the CRO needs to be intimately familiar with the detail of such arrangements so that he or she understands where deal blockers may exist and the levers that can be pulled to move the process along.

The key financial stakeholders are usually senior lenders, bondholders and, increasingly, mezzanine funders and guarantee providers. There are, however, other key financial stakeholders who must also be included in the process, with a similar investment of effort to understand their agendas and secure their support. These may include:

- **Trade insurance companies**. Through their penetration into the vendor community, trade insurers effectively consolidate what is otherwise a diverse class of creditors to a focused representation, with an increasingly important voice at the restructuring table.

- **Pension fund trustees**. Under the Pensions Act 2004, the powers of the Pensions Regulator have greatly increased and this has in turn increased significantly the negotiating leverage of pension fund trustees in any company with a significant final salary scheme deficit. It is likely that, in future, the trustees (and the Regulator) will be a significant stakeholder in most major UK restructuring negotiations and the restructuring leader and his or her advisers will have to address this added complexity through extensive consultation and negotiation. This will present particular challenges as most trustees are ill-equipped to deal with such negotiations, yet the Regulator has extensive powers that could lead to unreasonable positions being adopted.

- **Government departments.** With the growth of public–private initiative schemes and other gain share arrangements, government departments are having an increasing influence on the way in which the cake is shared when participant companies or government suppliers are restructured.

- **Equity**. Historically, once a company's senior debt was impaired, junior debt and equity holders were deemed to have lost all their economic interest and were not active participants in the restructuring process, other than where a single shareholder (such as a parent company) provided additional financial support in order to "stay in the game". Increasingly, equity providers are building protection into their investments, for example through shareholder agreements in private equity investments, which can provide significant negotiating leverage, irrespective of the pure economics of their position. The restructuring leader must achieve a balance between the demands of those with a true economic interest and the rights of other stakeholders, who may have little to lose but much to gain by using their leverage to take a piece of the cake. These "side show" negotiations can threaten to take over the restructuring process; it is the CRO's task to keep the restructuring "on track" through his or her judicious handling of the stakeholders.

*The case of Stolt Offshore SA illustrates the role of the CRO in managing and aligning stakeholder agendas to achieve a successful restructuring* (see Box 10.4).

---

**Box 10.4   Stakeholder Management and Restructuring at Stolt Offshore**

*(The background to the Stolt Offshore restructuring was described in Box 8.4)*

In the spring of 2003, Tom Ehret, a highly–respected industry executive, was appointed as CEO and was joined by a new CFO, Stuart Jackson. It quickly became apparent to Tom and Stuart that the situation at SOSA was far worse than they had been led to believe before joining the company. The "legacy" contracts were continuing to haemorrhage money, the business was under-capitalised, there were covenant breaches and a real risk of insolvency. SNSA, the parent company, had its own problems to contend with, including a US Department of Justice investigation into another of its subsidiaries and, under pressure from its own creditors, had publicly announced that it would not provide further funding to SOSA. As a contracting business, SOSA was heavily dependent on providing performance guarantees to its customers to secure new business, but its bank guarantee facilities were either fully utilised or had been withdrawn.

Tom and Stuart had made substantial progress in setting strategy and improving the operations but the state of the balance sheet was hindering further progress. The company's debt had soared to over $400 million, its gearing was over 300%, it was running short of liquidity and performance bonding facilities, and was in breach of its banking covenants. As there were 27 financial institutions with exposure to the company, concern was high, confidence was low and the debt was starting to trade. Many of the banks had lent to SOSA on the back of their relationships with the parent company, and felt badly let down when SNSA announced that it would not provide further support. Perhaps not surprisingly in the post-Enron era, corporate governance became the hottest issue, with huge pressure for Boardroom change.

A financial restructuring was inevitable but first the company needed to find someone to lead the process and leave management to focus on the critical operational turnaround. David Lovett and Laura Barlow of AlixPartners were appointed as Chief Restructuring Officers in November 2003. Their key task was to gain the support of a sceptical banking group by showing that the business had a viable future and that the right management was in place with the appropriate plans for recovery. Many of the banks had had no direct contact with the company hitherto. Communication was the key and a series of one-to-one meetings was held with each of the lenders, to listen to their concerns and start to develop a solution that would meet their objectives.

The meetings revealed that there was not only considerable scepticism among the banks towards the company, but also mistrust between the banks themselves. There was no standstill and banks with bilateral arrangements sought to achieve settlement ahead of other, syndicated facilities. The company was surviving from one covenant breach waiver to the next, with each waiver involving over 100 parties, and consuming enormous time, effort and expense. It was critical that the business move rapidly towards a permanent solution to provide a stable platform for its operational turnaround.

Finding a solution depended on responding to the stakeholders' concerns. The support of the lenders was critical to the company; in return, the creditors required changes in governance, such that the parent company's influence over SOSA was restricted and an independent Board was in place. Putting new performance guarantee facilities in place was also fundamental to the future viability of the business. The only facilities on offer were extremely expensive, but experienced CROs know that survival today is critical in order to live on and fight again tomorrow.

The senior creditors had commissioned a liquidation analysis, which appeared to support their instinct to seek recovery through a workout. The CROs concurred with the company's view that the best prospect of recovery was through a turnaround, to be supported by the introduction of new equity. The company then pursued an equity placement and subsequent rights issue that brought new money into the company and diluted the former parent's interests, thereby addressing the governance concerns of the creditors.

Within six months of the CROs' appointment, SOSA completed an $844 million financial restructuring, including raising $165 million of new equity, debt conversion, amendments to its existing facilities and securing $100 million of additional performance bonding capacity – critical to its future viability. Governance was also addressed; SOSA was de-consolidated from its former parent and an independent Board was constituted. Throughout the process, the CROs maintained a clear agenda to support the company and restore it to viability, seeking to build and retain stakeholder support without acceding to the agenda of any one class or institution.

In November 2004, SOSA's recovery was completed through a $350 million refinancing, repaying all its existing lenders at par. From the brink of failure in 2003, with its debt trading at a substantial discount, SOSA's turnaround was reflected in a six-fold increase in market capitalisation, to over $1 billion.

## Understanding the Corporate's Needs

The company itself is, of course, central to the restructuring; without a viable business going forward, there is no point in attempting a restructuring. This seems obvious, yet once the restructuring negotiations are underway, the needs of the company can seem to be forgotten as the other stakeholders each focus on securing the best possible outcome for themselves. An assessment of the company's liquidity needs, which is often carried out by reporting accountants or other specialist turnaround advisers, is the starting point for understanding the needs of the business – but not enough by itself. The restructuring leader needs to ensure that the longer-term requirements of the business are addressed. The number one objective of the restructuring should always be to establish a stable capital structure, commensurate with the enterprise value and cash-generating capacity of the revitalised business. These requirements should be reflected in the business plan for the company, which will document where the company is, where it plans to go and how it plans to get there. The plan must be credible with regard to its circumstances and the market it serves, and the restructuring leader or CRO will be closely involved in developing the plan and articulating it to the stakeholders. The plan must be credible and achievable, not aspirational – whether or not this meets the value requirements of the stakeholder audience. Managing the expectations of the stakeholders as regards the corporate's needs and capabilities is a critical part of the restructuring leader's role, as exemplified in the case study on Boxclever (see Box 10.5).

---

**Box 10.5    Understanding Corporate Needs at Boxclever Ltd**

AlixPartners was appointed by the Board as lead financial and turnaround adviser to Boxclever Ltd, a UK TV rental business. The company operated a very cash-generative business model but the customer base was in steady decline due to the gradual shift from TV rental to outright ownership in the UK market. Boxclever had approximately £800 million of debt, which had been placed two years earlier, through a complex securitisation arrangement, with three financial institutions – one German, one Canadian and one French. At the time of AlixPartners' appointment, it was becoming clear that the financial model that had been the base for the securitisation was flawed and that the company could not generate the cashflows required to service the securitisation structure.

The key task was to determine the company's true debt capacity, based on a realistic and achievable business plan. The first pass of the plan was produced in a very short period and indicated that the company was unable to fund the debt burden. Indeed, it was only able to fund approximately 25% of the securitisation debt.

This was a difficult pill for the lenders to swallow and they granted a standstill agreement while reporting accountants checked the plan, and management were charged with "sharpening their pencil" since what was an offer was "not good enough"! Despite considerable spend on further professional fees and the examination of many alternative scenarios, the funding level that could be serviced changed little.

As is often the case, it was the task of AlixPartners as restructuring advisers to communicate the bad news to the financial institutions and start to close the reality gap. It was clear that a solution was needed that would reflect the reality of Boxclever's debt capacity and business potential. Eventually, the lenders exited by selling down their positions to two US-based hedge funds.

## Co-ordinating Advisers

Loan documentation is normally drawn up to enable the financial stakeholders to take advice with regard to their loans or exposures at the expense of the company. Even where this is not the case, it will become a condition of support as soon as covenant waivers or additional funding are required. Enormous fees are incurred by advisers on behalf of their clients but these are all paid from the capital of the distressed company. The company management will typically have little experience of what is involved or what is required and there is the risk of considerable duplication of work or unneccessary activity as each group of stakeholders engages its own team of advisers. The restructuring leader will be familiar with these situations and it is part of his or her role to co-ordinate the advisers, to minimise disruption to the company from multiple demands for information and to reduce the cost involved by avoiding duplication of effort.

Each of the principal stakeholder groups will normally engage advisers who are typically lawyers and financial advisers, such as reporting accountants or specialist investment bankers. Each of these advisers has an important role to play in the restructuring process and may take a leadership role in certain activities.

*Reporting Accountants*

These advisers play an important role in determining the current financial position and helping to review and interpret the proposed business plan. This financial due diligence is critical to enable all stakeholders to receive an objective view of the business value and potential options, as the starting point for restructuring negotiations. Historically, some reporting accountants also played a leading role in negotiations, usually on behalf of the senior lenders, but recent changes in the regulatory environment post-Enron, and the rise of the CRO, have made this less common.

It would be unusual for each creditor class to engage its own reporting accountant, although it may occur where there is significant inter-class conflict and a reluctance to share the analysis, or where financial interpretation is critical to determining the future structure of the company. The reporting accountant is normally retained by the company at the instigation of the senior lenders and makes their work available to each other class of financial stakeholder. The exception is the liquidation analysis, which will normally only be made available to one class of stakeholder as this has considerable influence on their negotiating position. The restructuring leader usually works closely with the reporting accountants to ensure that their work is factually correct, does not misrepresent the company and objectively reflects the value potential of a consensual restructuring.

## Lawyers

Lawyers are normally engaged by each class of stakeholder and play a critical role since they advise on the architecture of the battlefield, tease out the weaknesses in the other players' positions and advise on how their clients can camouflage or repair the weaknesses in their own positions. Restructuring is a specialist area of law and some firms act predominantly for one particular creditor class, such as US bondholders or senior lenders, while others "cross the table" and act for different sides in different transactions.

The lawyers play a critical role in preparing for the restructuring negotiations and in documenting agreements as they emerge. Some also play a key role in negotiating on behalf of their clients. During the documentation stage, we observe many drafting techniques and ploys to make the most out of what has been achieved during the negotiations. The lawyer to the company will work closely with the restructuring leader throughout the restructuring process.

*Financial Advisers*

Financial advisers, who are drawn from specialist departments within certain investment banks or turnaround and corporate finance boutiques, complete the team. If a financial restructuring involves a listed company, the raising or swapping of complex financial instruments or access to the capital markets, for example through a rescue rights issue, it is usual for the company to retain its own specialist investment bank. The investment banks will also operate in an advisory capacity for a particular stakeholder class, often leading negotiations on behalf of a bondholder or creditor committee. The leadership role of these specialised investment banking departments is discussed in more detail in the case studies on Marconi and British Energy. (see Boxes 10.6 and 10.7)

---

**Box 10.6    Financial Restructuring of Marconi Plc**

The background to the Marconi restructuring was set out in Chapter 4. It was one of the most complicated financial restructurings ever seen in the UK, requiring two court-approved schemes of arrangement and fundamental changes to the Board, management, operations and capital structure.

Lazard acted as lead financial advisers to the Board throughout the restructuring. At its peak, Marconi was valued at over £30 billion and had over £4 billion of financial debt. On completion of the restructuring and debt-for-equity swap, £5.6 billion of claims had been cancelled, including £3.4 billion of bank and bond debt and the equity in the new company was valued at £300 million.

Richard Stables of Lazard says that agreeing a valuation and a realistic level of part restructuring indebtedness were the key to achieving a consensual restructuring. Against such a fundamental change in value, he saw Lazard's role as being "a consensus builder around a valuation which required both art and science".

The restructuring was implemented via two Creditor Schemes of Arrangement (at the corporate and Plc levels). A key creditor demand was that the financial restructuring should not be conditional on a Plc shareholder vote. In return, the Board was insistent that the shareholders should retain some residual part of the new equity plus some upside potential. The restructuring was effected by a debt-for-equity swap leading to a substantial debt reduction. Following the restructuring, bondholders, banks and other credtiors received 99.5% of the equity of the newly formed Marconi Corporation. Original shareholders received 0.5%, plus "out-of-the-money" warrants over a further 5% of new equity.

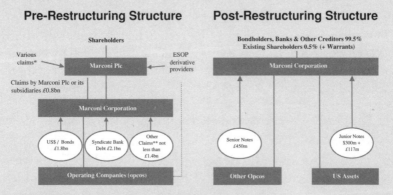

**Pre-Restructuring Structure**   **Post-Restructuring Structure**

*Including guarantees of bank and bond debt.

Over 18 months elapsed from initial negotiations with the banks to final completion of the restructuring. The roles of the restructuring adviser (Lazard and CRO John Talbot of Talbot Hughes) were critical in building consensus and maintaining support for the company. Their tasks included: persuading the Board to recognise the reality of the situation and the consequent and dramatic shift in economic interest in the business; managing communications and negotiations with the key stakeholder groups; determining an appropriate structure that maximised stakeholders recoveries while leaving sufficient liquidity in the business to meet its future needs; and project managing an immensely complex process – as reflected in a scheme document that ran to over 1,000 pages.

The debt was trading actively throughout the negotiations and numerous issues – from settlement of claims on a complex swap contract on the employee share ownership scheme to dealing with the requirements of the US pensions regulator – threatened, at times, to de-rail the process and force the company into insolvency proceedings. Without the leadership of its key advisers and the credibility and expertise they brought to a deeply discredited company, it is unlikely that Marconi would have survived.

---

**Box 10.7    Advising Bondholders at British Energy**

In December 2002, Close Brothers was retained as restructuring adviser to the bondholders of British Energy (BE) following the announcement of its restructuring proposals on 28 November 2002. British Energy is the largest electricity generator in the UK. It owns and operates eight nuclear power stations with approximately 20% of the UK's generating capacity.

- The Government-backed restructuring proposal included the following key points

  - The Government (HMG) agreed to underwrite a new Nuclear Liability Fund (NLF), which will be part-funded by BE, with the NLF receiving 65% of cash flow generated by British Energy going forward. The NLF will assume all existing and future nuclear liabilities in respect of the nuclear fleet.

  - British Nuclear Fuels Plc (BNFL) entered into heads of terms for revised contracts with respect to front and back-end fuel-related services to British Energy.

  - Overseas investments in North America nuclear power plants to be sold.

  - £700m of new bonds plus new equity to be shared among creditors (including bondholders).

- Creditors entered into standstill arrangements and heads of terms for the restructuring on 14 February 2003 to work towards a formal binding agreement on the restructuring between the company and its creditors by 30 September 2003 in accordance with the agreed heads of terms.

- On 1 October 2003, the company announced that its creditors had reached binding agreement, subject to EU Commission approval of the State Aid being provided by the UK Government as part of the deal, and subject to obtaining sufficient creditor support, including 75% agreement of bondholders by value.

- Under the terms of the restructuring, bondholders will receive £154.1 million of new bonds at par and 51% of the new equity in British Energy following implementation of the restructuring.

Close Brothers worked exclusively for the bondholders. Their role included:

- Quickly bringing together a cohesive bondholder group.

- Bringing other creditors together to agree a response to British Energy's restructuring proposal.

- Negotiating heads of terms on behalf of the bondholders.

Close Brothers worked with British Energy and other creditors to achieve a formal binding agreement of the restructuring.

Peter Collini, Managing Director of Riverhill Partners, a boutique corporate advisory firm, identifies the following key attributes for success, based on his experience of advising clients on restructuring coding.

- The ability to gain the trust of and influence the Board in highly stressful circumstances.

- A frank and open approach with lenders and the Board and a highly refined sense of timing/presentation to achieve a rational response to a given set of circumstances.

- Flexible approach and creative solutions to deal with constantly changing situations.

- Helping management to retain a sense of proportion in highly unstable situations and trying to buy time to consider matters properly.

- Early recognition of the need to bring on board other resource input as required (for example, executive change, a CRO, operational support, enhanced financial reporting).

Martin Gudgeon of Close Brothers, who advises both debtor and creditor groups on restructuring, summarises the key attributes that specialist investment banks bring to the restructuring process as follows:

- Understanding the secondary market.

- Understanding the market view of the creditors.

- Assessing whether the company has the right management team (do they need to be helped by the appointment of a CRO?).

- Understanding the exit plan.

- Always having a "Plan B" in any negotiation.

## Leading Restructuring Negotiations

Having agreed a standstill (where possible), developed a detailed understanding of the stakeholder positions and corporate needs, and corralled the advisers, the restructuring leader now takes centre stage to lead the restructuring negotiations and develop a permanent solution for the company. It is logical for the CRO, as the representative of the company, to lead all negotiations between the company and the various stakeholders, since the company is the final counter-party to all arrangements (and is the only party that cannot therefore be conflicted). There is inevitably considerable tension and a lack of trust between the parties, given the likely background of unfulfilled promises, blame and counter-blame. The restructuring leader has no such baggage and brings independence and objectivity to the process. As "honest broker", the leader will use his or her experience and negotiating skills to the maximum, knowing when to be hard-nosed and when to accommodate demands, but always remaining focused on the ultimate goal of achieving a lasting agreement.

In Chapter 6 we described the parties typically participating in the negotiations, and we can use the analogy of a dinner table (Figure 10.1) to illustrate the key participants. Inevitably, all those involved at the financial restructuring table seek to obtain as large a slice of the cake as they can, seeking to show that their investment is not impaired or that the impairment is as small as possible (in the case of par lenders) or to maximise their return if they have acquired debt at a discount.

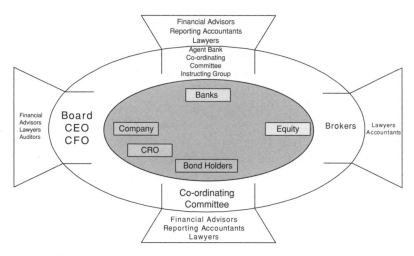

**Figure 10.1** The Financial Restructuring Dinner Party.

The restructuring must be based on a realistic business plan and assessment of future debt capacity and a balance sheet that properly reflects the values of the assets available to the company.

In Corporate Turnaround, a feature that we observed in troubled companies was described as the "Reality Gap" – that is, the gap between the perception of (or desire for) value in the company and its true value, based on the varying levels of knowledge of the facts between the company and its creditors. Managing that gap is a critical part of stakeholder management, particularly as the gap also exists between different financial institutions both within and between classes. The leader needs to be aware of these gaps and allow sufficient time for the various participants to "get up to speed" and manage their internal communication of the new reality. Like a good dinner party host, the restructuring leader must manage the tempo of the discussion and ensure that no participant feels ignored or left behind. Without this, there is less chance of a restructuring proposal being received favourably by all those affected by it; while the reality gap persists it may fall considerably short of their expectations of its value. Facing reality and the consequent impairment of investments can be a bitter pill to swallow for many institutions, and the restructuring leader may seek to mitigate this by building upside opportunities (such as warrants) into the restructuring proposal to help institutions to manage their positions.

Each class of stakeholder is normally represented by a formal or informal co-ordinating committee, appointed by the other members of their class to negotiate on its behalf. The restructuring leader will deal predominantly with the leaders who emerge in each of the co-ordinating committees. The committee chairs will have their own leadership challenges since they need to carry all the banks/bondholders (or a predetermined majority, depending on the original loan documentation) with their proposed position. Within each class, some creditors will have bought in below par and therefore have a different view of value and acceptability, some will be represented by the relationship bankers who made the original loans, whereas others will have passed the account to their workout departments, who will have different incentives and agendas. There will be a differing degree of knowledge and understanding within the classes and the restructuring leader needs to understand the dynamics within each group and support the co-ordinating committee as well as he or she can, since negotiations may collapse if the co-ordinating committee fails to carry its constituent members.

If a syndicate of banks is involved, the agent bank usually plays a pivotal role and sits on or leads the co-ordinating committee, together with representatives from the lenders with the biggest exposure. However, as debt is traded, the landscape changes. Not many debt traders are interested in taking on – or have the back-office facilities to take on – the onerous task of agent. Thus the situation can arise – as at Eurotunnel – in which the agent bank has sold down all its debt and has no economic exposure, but no one else will take over the agent's role. In such circumstances, the agent's ability to influence a particular course of action is diminished by its lack of economic interest in the outcome, increasing the pressure on the restructuring leader to keep the other lenders "in line".

As this "caravan" of principals and advisers proceeds, with all costs being borne by the distressed company, the restructuring leader needs to:

• Propose and achieve buy-in from the parties to a timetable that balances the company's desire for an early resolution with the stakeholders' requirements to get up to speed and manage internal communications and approvals processes.

- Manage the parties' progress through the timetable, remembering that every deal has its own tempo; to move too fast can frustrate progress but to move too slowly often incurs more cost and more frustration.

- Propose an outline restructuring plan. This is normally documented in a "draft participation agreement". The document expands during the negotiation period and will include the "gives and gets" of all participants. When eventually agreed, it will become the framework agreement from which the definitive legal documentation is drafted. The document needs to focus on addressing the commercial issues and requirements but must also address any critical legal points that may otherwise de-rail the final legal documentation.

Development of the draft participation agreement requires a lot of listening and understanding by the leader, who often acts here as an honest broker. His or her knowledge of each party's position, rights and options is critical to a successful outcome. Some stakeholders will "hold out" at different stages and the leader needs to be balanced in his or her response to such positions. Sometimes others have to give in, and at other times their bluff has to be called. At times the leader might seek the support of other stakeholders, who may have other institutional relationships with an errant party, to bring pressure to bear through those relationships and thus find a solution to seemingly intractable problems.

It is usually not sensible to concede to "hold out" creditors (those holding out for better terms) since this can result in a "domino effect" with others following suit. The restructuring leader's knowledge of the financial institutions and the individuals concerned is critical in unlocking a deadlocked situation. The leader must also be prepared to use every means at his disposal to move towards a solution. For example, he might instruct the lawyers acting for the company to investigate potential action against and remedy from such creditors, in the event that their behaviour results in collapse of the restructuring and loss of value to others. The leader will use such information judiciously to achieve his or her negotiating goals.

In theory, once a participation agreement is reached, the restructuring leader has largely completed his or her task and the lawyers can take over and draft the substantive agreements. Unfortunately, this often proves to be too optimistic and the parties continue to spar right up to signing, hence the need for the leader to continue to drive the process to a tight timetable until the close.

Although consensual out-of-court restructurings normally mitigate loss substantially (certainly compared to the alternative of liquidation) and provide a platform for value restoration through implementation of a turnaround, the completion meetings are often sombre affairs. Most stakeholders will feel as if they have been beaten into submission by other classes of creditor, their own class and the company, yet all will be relieved that there remains an opportunity to rebuild economic interest. Success, to some extent, is defined as "each stakeholder feeling he or she conceded a little more than expected in order to reach a conclusion".

Against this background the leader must not, to use Calvyn Gardner's expression, be one who lets excellence be the enemy of the good. The solution will have been the result of many trade-offs and side deals, and although something better could nearly always have been done on a particular item, there will usually not be a better solution to the whole. The leader needs to have the experience and courage to know when to stop the discussions and move forward.

# Appendix

## Society of Turnaround Professionals

T HE SOCIETY OF TURNAROUND PROFESSIONALS (STP) IS THE
only UK-based professional body accrediting the highest quality
turnaround professionals, increasingly recognised and required by
the stakeholder community, including the major UK clearing banks.
It is an independent non-profit making body governed by a board of
nine non-executive directors, and run by a full-time chief executive.

STP's principal services are:

- Accreditation of independent executives, together with advisers
  and stakeholder representatives, who demonstrate high-quality
  experience in a turnaround.

- Increasing the knowledge and success of a turnaround by providing education, training and the provision of practical information
  notes for those engaged in turnaround work.

- Free one-day consultancy service by STP accredited independent
  executives for company directors wishing to discuss potential difficulties in the strictest confidence.

- Regulation of STP accredited turnaround professionals.

- Networking and education opportunities for members via regular
  meetings in London and key centres around the UK, including
  Birmingham, Bristol, Edinburgh, Leeds and Manchester.

- Free Turnaround Executive Introduction Service to enable companies and stakeholders to identify accredited independent executives for particular assignments.

- Lobbying Government and others on matters affecting the success of corporate recovery, such as the recent Pensions Act and its "Moral Hazard" clauses.

- Annual Turnaround Awards Dinner to recognise excellence in the field of turnaround.

- Annual Turnaround Conference to contribute to the future development of turnaround.

STP is widely supported by leading UK institutions dedicated to the successful restoration of corporate success, including the major clearing banks (Barclays, HBoS, HSBC and Royal Bank of Scotland); the large accounting practices (Deloittes, Ernst & Young, KPMG, PWC, Kroll and Numerica); principal legal firms (Ashurst, Berwin Leighton Paisner, Freshfields Bruckhaus Deringer and Travers Smith); turnaround financiers and service providers (Alchemy, Burdale, Eurofactor, Gordon Bros, Hilco, Independent Trustee Services, Kelso, Rutland, Venture Finance); and a turnaround boutique (AlixPartners).

Further information is available from STP on +44 (0) 20 7566 4222 or at www.stp-uk.org.

# Index

*Index compiled by Annette Musker*